Coffee Pot Journal

A Year's Journey in Faith

by

Irena Milloy

Published in the UK by:
Avon Court Publishing
18, Adolphus Road, LONDON N4 2AZ

Copyright © 2008 Irena Milloy

I would like to thank all those who have helped me to bring this book to publication. To all my brothers and sisters in faith who have encouraged me, especially Peter, to Cynthia for her proof reading and to Gareth for his tuition in how to get published.

Foreword

Through my involvement with quiet days and retreats I have had the privilege of giving people the space 'just to be', of encouraging people to come empty in order to be filled. Much has been written by far greater luminaries than I about the importance of stopping before the voice of God can be heard.

The Reverend Dr Martin Israel wrote:

'God is eternally present; it is we who are so seldom at home in ourselves to receive him.'

Many of the poems and thoughts in this journal have been elements in days of spiritual exploration and asked for afterwards by various individuals, so it seemed right to share the whole year's journey with those who take their quiet time alone.

I hope you will find inspiration, laughter and something to think about over the coming days and months as you share my eclectic musings.

January 1st

Another New year Lord.

Another resolution to pay more attention to my spiritual life.

Another promise of set quiet times.

Another commitment to getting through the whole of my quarterly bible reading notes and not just the first few weeks…..

Oh ! and I will address my charitable giving and try to curb my non essential spending…..and of course I will make more time to get in touch with friends and family where I've let things slip.

Heavenly Father, instead of setting out what **I** intend to do, knowing I will most certainly fail, thank you that I can face this New Year knowing the certainty of your love.

Knowing that however weak my efforts or however heroic, your love is unconditional.

Thank you for the monumental knowledge that whatever this year holds I am not alone but walk the road with you beside me.

January 2nd

I am so aware that in this season of excess there are many around the world with little or nothing. I accept that there is not much I can do physically but Lord I am grateful for all that we, as a nation, have in this relatively stable part of the world. Our tears will not quench the thirst of those oppressed by drought or starvation but I pray for a growing appreciation of simple things and a commitment by all of us with plenty to share more fairly your resources between the haves and the have nots.

January 3rd

Father, what an amazing thought that you are

all-powerful

invincible

unstoppable

supreme

in fact omnipotent.

What an even more amazing thought that you care about each and every one of us and that through the power of the Holy Spirit we can have access to your

collective

total

complete

unanimous

universal greatness.

Help me to know more of these mysteries as I grow in faith.

January 4th

I am tired today, perhaps the result of a couple of busy weeks.

Lord as I chastise myself for being pathetic and self indulgent I remember those whose strength is sapped by the strain of looking after someone who is unwell, whose life is one long round of caring, whose day and night are as one.

I hold them all before you; I bring them and lift them up for your blessing.

May they have some small thing happen today which will alleviate their responsibility for a while; maybe a phone call or an unexpected visitor. Maybe a piece of music on the radio or a television programme for which they could take time out of their routines to sit and enjoy. Something which makes them feel your cool hand on their brow.

Lord Jesus who cares for us, I pray for the carers.   Heb.12:12

January 5th

I found a snow-drop this morning and the little, tiny, intricate, perfect structure made my heart sing. Soon there will be others and hopefully the plants, which I have built up over the years, will make a perfect white carpet. There will be a drift of flawless beauty for me to enjoy. In the Victorian language of flowers snowdrops meant 'I make another bid for your love' and I think how wonderful that the love of God is not part of a bidding war but given with such generosity to all who are open to receive it.

Help me to reflect your love to someone today.

January 6th

Epiphany - Three Kings Day.!

Glorious Lord Jesus today we celebrate the visit of the Magi to the infant Christ, the first Gentiles to hail you as King.

Throughout the church this day is dedicated to Mission and Lord I dedicate myself, afresh, to help in the mission of Christ the King.

To share the gospel of your Good News.

To share the newness and hope which your birth brought.

To have the courage of my convictions and seize opportunities as they arise to tell others of you.

Lord uphold me as I step out in faith like the Three Wise Men did and Lord keep me safe if, in the course of my mission, I should have to travel into unknown territory.

In the name of Jesus.

January 7th

One week into this New Year and I am still optimistic that I will fulfil some of my resolutions; only another fifty one weeks to go!

Oh Lord one day at a time and how many times a day do I call on you for the right word, the right direction, to know when to get involved, to know when to keep quiet?

Father thank you for showing me that the daunting task of a year of over enthusiastic resolution can be broken down into bite size pieces. Thank you that in taking the days one at a time I can begin to feel capable of keeping some dedication to my spiritual growth and knowing more of you.

Lord, you taught us to 'take no thought for the morrow for the morrow shall take thought for the things of itself.' and so I pray that I will continue to live my life in a daily walk with you, listening, learning and growing in grace.

Matt. 6:34

January 8th

Heavenly Father, Thank you.

I have such a list of things to pray for and yet I know that I don't need to read a multitude of requests and intercessions out to you because you already have every situation covered.

So, with a sincere faith I simply hold all these people and their problems in my heart and give thanks and praise to you for your great glory.......

Heavenly Father, Loving Lord, Thank you.

Heavenly Father, Loving Lord, Thank you.

January 9th

I heard of someone today who is an 'epistemologist' a word which I confess I had to look up to fully understand its meaning.

OED def:- Theory of Knowledge - the branch of philosophy that studies the nature of knowledge, in particular its foundations, scope and validity.'

Much of the debate in this field has focused on analysing the nature of knowledge and how it relates to similar notions such as truth, belief and justification. In other words, epistemology primarily addresses the following questions: "What is knowledge?", "How is knowledge acquired?", and "What do people know?

I acknowledge now Lord that I would be ill equipped to speak to a person of this academic discipline about you because I cannot be analytical enough regarding my faith. I cannot talk in absolutes about your love which I know empowers my every waking moment.

I cannot prove, as truth, your capacity except when relating it to my own personal experience.

Father lead me to think deeply about my faith yet allow me to rest gratefully in my personal understanding at this stage on my journey.

January 10th

Where is heaven Lord? The clouds today are perfect and have drawn my eyes 'heavenward' several times.

Our childish faith that 'up' is heaven and 'down' is hell still prevails in me even when, as an adult, and with the march of technology, I know that those sentiments are purely allegorical.

Isn't heaven a state of total perfection, of nirvana, of ethereal oneness with you, nowhere and everywhere?

Lord does it matter that I still look up to the sky when I think about you and angels and all goodness?

Preserve in me the trust of my childlike faith Lord Jesus, especially when I can't make sense of what is going on in your beautiful world.

January 11th

Father forgive me.

I hate letting you down and yet I get so cross. I don't stop to think 'what would Jesus do' I just boil over first and think second.

I get so irritated by people's stupidity.

Who says they're stupid?

Well I do of course.

Who are *they*?

Anyone who gets in my way when I'm driving and *they* do stupid things;

when I'm in the supermarket and *they* do stupid things;

when I make a phone call and get a stupid response.

Lord preserve me from stupid people!

No Lord; please help me to be more patient, more kindly, more gentle and to reflect you and your example in all my everyday meetings.

Lord, save me from myself. Jas.2 ch1:19

January 12th

Father of all, I pray for peace in the world and yet I doubt that it can ever be. Mankind seems hell bent on a path of destruction in the name of its own particular vanities and conceit; very often in the name of God.

To take your name and turn it into something as vile as war is beyond my understanding and yet the conflicts rage on.

How can I help?

What can I do?

Lord with your grace, help us all, in our own areas of this world, to reflect your love and gospel of peace and reconciliation.

In the smallest ways help us to treasure your kingdom here on earth and to know your peace.

Blessed be the peace makers.

January 13th

I saw the book title 'Deeper into God' on the bookshelf and know that I need to make time to do just that.

To allow myself the time to switch off from the everyday, to allow myself time to submit to your will and give the Holy Spirit free reign to reveal more of your mystery to me.

I want to go deeper into God so that God may go deeper into me.

That the very core of my being might be touched and brought to an inner awareness as yet unexplored.

That my soul might be washed by the water of Pentecost and that the revelations of that power might be manifest in me.

Lord hear me, Lord graciously hear me.

January 14th

Father God, who through your amazing gift of Jesus, brought us the power of the Holy Spirit, come close to me today.

I enter your presence with empty hands and an open heart.

Hands which lay open in my lap with nothing but expectation and a heart that waits on you.

I ask nothing but that I listen for your voice.

I ask nothing but that I hear your voice.

Lord the only sound is my breathing, the only feeling one of a growing awareness of peace and love.

Father God, who, through your amazing gift of Jesus brought us the power of the Holy Spirit, come close to me today, that as I sit in your presence you will meet me.

January 15th

Dear Lord, short days and long nights, less time to do what has to be done and more time to lie awake worrying about it. How can I be so much more hopeless at accomplishing everything in the depths of winter than during the long balmy days of summer?

How come I seem to be so less efficient at time management, there are still 24 hours in the day?

Hours haven't been pruned from the clock.

If I am making excuses for wasting time I'm sorry.

If I'm making excuses for enjoying not having to fill time with chores, thank you.

January 16th

Father as I ask for your forgiveness in my daily prayers, I rest safe in the assurance that you do indeed forgive my sins.

Am I so forgiving to those who I consider have sinned against me?

Help me to search my heart, to dig out all the grudges and grievances which I hold so close; all the unholy baggage which I justify still hanging onto, which I actually enjoy getting out and chewing over every now and then.

Lord show me the flaws in my self righteous indignation, which I can so competently reason hanging onto.

How can I, with such sincere longing, ask for your forgiveness yet be so insincere?

When I say the words 'as we forgive those who sin against us' help me to truly mean them.

January 17th

Loving Lord Jesus may my mouth sing forth your praise today.

May nothing I utter be anything other than a psalm of thanksgiving for my life in all its fullness.

Lord before I even begin to be negative help me to turn thoughts around and, if not to exactly find the positive, then to appreciate where I am in a situation compared to millions of others.

Help me then to remain silent and focused only on you until I can sing your praise once more.

January 18th

Lord it is cold today,
and grey
and damp
and really just a nothing sort of a day.
The house looks dim,
the garden looks as though it has given up on itself,
the news is full of awfulness
and I feel totally dragged down with everything.

I rest in your love and pray that even in this morass of grey self pity I might find the motivation to get on with something worthwhile.

I rest in your love and pray that from this pathetic state I will be led to a deeper understanding of what you want from me, of what I can or should be doing for you.

January 19th

Thank you for yesterday Lord.

Today, outside and inside is the same grey nothingness. Even the dog doesn't want to go out of a walk but thank you for yesterday.

I dealt with my feelings of gloom.

I had omitted to realise the opportunities that an enforced day in doors might offer…until too much of it had passed in self obsessed introspection.

So Lord thank you for today and for the luxury of being able to stay in my warm home and do some writing which I have been putting off for too long.

Thank you for time to listen to music and the radio whilst I go through the day and Lord,

> thank you for the deeply treasured knowledge that you will be here with me.

January 20th

Week-end breaks and city escapes!
holiday brochures are flying in,
Go to the mountains or down to the sea,
dream of dodging the factory's din?
Colour supplements all about travel,
value for money and two for one places,
so many details to read and unravel.
so many seemingly 'perfect' spaces.
Paradise beckons a few hours away,
it's 'cheaper than chips' as the TV says.
Take a cruise to the Baltic or try Marrakesh,
get away from it all; we've got a crèche
and running buffet - you can eat all day,
sail, fly or drive,
so many details
Oh Lord I pray
What happened to holy-days?

January 21st

Father God, thank you that I can come in trust and faith to a place where you will meet me and hear me and help me.

That through my prayers I can draw close to you and know that you are close to me.

That through my acknowledgement of my weakness, I can have some perception of your immense power and strength.

Father it is sufficient for me to know that you will support me, that you will hold and protect me, whatever comes my way today and that through the power of the Holy Spirit I will have whatever I need; the right words, the right thoughts, the right attitude to not just cope but to triumph for you.

Father God I give you thanks and praise.

January 22nd

My friend said
    'be kind to yourself today'
and I came away thanking God for her.
My friend said
    'be kind to yourself today'
and I came away with a quiet peace.

The peace which she asked God to put into my heart.
The peace which the love and prayers of a friend can bring about.

I will be kind to myself today.
I will not fight to carry on with so much
in my head to clutter and cloud the key issues.
I will be kind to myself today.
I will come into His presence and bring
all my turmoil to Him, I will pray.

My friend said
    'be kind to yourself today'
and I am going to stay quiet and still
in the company of Him whose will for me
is to receive His grace.

January 23rd

Peace.

The peace which the world cannot give.

Loving Lord Jesus I pray that you will show me how to seek that peace, that you will help me to access that peace.

Lord I know that in that peace I will find myself close to you and I crave that opportunity.

I thirst for the cool waters which will baptise me in your all encompassing presence.

I cry for my inner turmoil to be stilled and my body to be at rest.

I know that until I do you the courtesy of making time, you can never truly give me what I seek.

Please help me to rationalise all that is unimportant in my life.

Help me to remove the obstacles which prevent me from having time to come to you.

Please enable me to come into your presence with time to experience your peace.

January 24th

Father of all, I come in quiet reverence.

I am grateful for the revelation through yesterday's prayer, that I must make time to come and be with you in open expectation if I am to have an increased awareness of your presence and power.

Thank you for this time and as I sit in stillness help me to free my mind of anything other than you.

That I may dwell only on you

and the faith which I have in you

and the love which I have for you.

Come Holy Sprit and breathe the new life of Christ's gospel into me.

Come Holy Spirit and breathe the new life of Christ into me.

Come Holy Spirit and breathe new life into me.

Come Holy Spirit and breathe into me.

Come Holy Spirit.

January 25th

It's the Feast of the Conversion of St Paul today Lord and I think of the way in which the Gospel of love was brought to Europe by him. We may never know the conversions which follow from the chance conversations we have with people and few experiences will be as Damascene as St Paul's but give me the opportunities to sow those seeds for you.

Give me the right words to share your love with people I meet and enable me to tell them about the promise of your everlasting tenderness and forgiveness.

Unlike our gardens we may never be there at the harvest of the seeds we sow for you. We may never see the final flowering of those tender shoots of faith which we water and feed as we pass in and out of people's lives. We probably won't observe their acceptance of you as Lord or see them acknowledge the Holy Spirit in their lives.

None the less Father may I never shy away from the opportunity to share the Good News of you with others.

January 26th

Oh Lord it was lovely this morning by the lake with the dog. The weak winter sun illuminated the dead grasses and reeds and threw their reflections onto the water. The cobwebs were still heavy with dew and glistened like strings of precious stones in a necklace. My breath came out in great puffs of steam which seemed to rejoice in its liberation before dissipating into the general air around me. The dog splashed in and out of the water swimming for sticks, oblivious to the cold; only determined to enjoy the wonder of the time we were out. I saw other dog walkers and we exchanged greetings, everyone seemingly lifted by the little bit of sunshine and able to appreciate the new day. Why am I telling you all this? You were there with me and I was thanking you all the time I was out. Well, I am grateful and I love being in this world of yours so thank you again.

January 27th

Reach out to me Lord
in my lonely times,
in my worried times,
in my unsure times.
Reach out to me Lord
hold me and
let me hear you say
Rest in my love
my love is sufficient.
Reach out to me Lord
in my ungraciousness,
in my ungratefulness,
in my petulance.
Reach out to me Lord,
touch me and
let me hear you say
'Do not be afraid, I am your God
let nothing terrify you.
I will make you strong and help you,
I will protect and save you.'   Is 41:10

January 28th

Father I am thinking about people working for you in our towns and cities, working on the streets with the unlovely and unclean; except of course to you they are neither unlovely nor unclean but are as precious as any one of the rest of us.

I am in awe of their dedication and compassion, their ability in the face of such abject misery to work with humour and good nature. I am made uncomfortable by their willingness to put their own lives in danger and discomfort on the uncertain night time city pavements.

We are not all called to do this work but we are commanded to uphold each other in prayer. So, Father, bless, guard and protect all in your service on the streets today and make me aware of my own reaction to those for whom life has not been so comfortable or kind.

January 29th

'Jesus moved with compassion.' Mk1:41

Lord increase in me the capacity for compassion I pray.

Teach me how to demonstrate your virtues of sympathy and concern, kindness and consideration.

Show me how to respond rather than react
and let that response be full of your love and generosity.

I ask it in your name Lord.

January 30th

It is foggy today, visibility is poor and without good reason to go out it is probably better, safer, to stay at home.

Father help me to understand the difference between being careful and being cowardly, between being sensibly cautious and hiding behind excuses for not doing something.

Father grant me the skill of discernment and the courage to act in situations where I might take the easy option to turn a blind eye.

Lord it might be foggy outside but help me to use this time to come to you and gain a greater vision of your purpose for my life.

January 31st

'This is the message from the one who is holy and true, he has the key that belonged to David and when he opens a door no-one can close it.' Rev.3:7

Thank you Lord Jesus for knocking on the door of my life until I heard and responded and thank you for loving me more than can I ever really know.

February 1st

Father God I give you thanks for the writers and compilers of bible notes; for the insights which they share with us, deepening our understanding of your word.

Help me to learn from them and to retain their teaching so that I can pass on to someone else the truth of your earthly power and supreme dedication to us all.

Open the eyes and minds of all who use these notes in a search for your essence.

Wipe away the scales of cynicism which attempt to rationalise teachings seemingly improbable or impossible in today's world.

At the start of this new month lead me deeper into my search for knowledge of you.

February 2nd

Candlemass Day, the Feast of Purification.

How powerful the light of a candle is and how symbolic.

We have candles for baptism; the Paschal candle at Easter; decoration on birthday cakes and special dinner tables; candles to carry prayer and supplication heavenward in quiet churches and chapels.

The Friday night menorah at dinner for Jewish families, the Advent ring; candles burning in remembrance beside headstones in the graveyard, scented candles burning to relax stress or ease worry.

Candles for every occasion!

Most importantly used to symbolise your light and life Lord Jesus,

'The Light of the World'

Lux aeterna.

February 3rd

Daffodils! My first daffodils are out and spring is in the air. They are beautiful and herald such promise for the rest of the year which, whilst not in doubt, is sometimes hard to envisage in the long dark days of winter.

Shall I pick some to have their beauty indoors or should I leave them out here to rejoice in their surroundings?

Lord help me to be uncomplicated like these flowers. Help me to just get on with 'being' and less with bothering about those things which get in the way of true loveliness.

Give me the strength to walk away from situations which do not need my interference. Give me the strength to ignore things which merely fuel my 'need to know' but which really are none of my business.

I will pick a few to have indoors to remind me of my prayer.

February 4th

To believe

Not to believe

To believe

Not to believe

To believe!

He loves me

He loves me not

He loves me

He loves me not

He loves me!

February 5th

I received more travel brochures today and a supplement about holiday insurance. How wonderful to know that every eventuality can be covered with a financial security blanket. That for a sum of money I can protect my self and my family against flood, fire, delayed flights, poor accommodation, injuries to body, mind or spirit; in fact insurance products to apparently fit every 'consumer need.'

What a peaceful holiday people will have with this fortress of provision around them!

Why aren't we sending out as many leaflets telling people about the promise of eternal life in you Lord? Why aren't we making more of an industry of telling the world about your security blanket of love, of forgiveness, of new life in the Spirit?

I guess industry doesn't have to mean huge commercial enterprise; it could just mean my efforts.

Father God, increase in me the industry to share my assurance of you, with others.

February 6th

'In the ways of justice and peace.'

We pray this week by week yet where is the justice or the peace?

There seems more jumble than justice, more muddle than mediation.

And peace! What peace?

Countries ripping into each other seeking their own agendas of 'justice and peace'.

What quality of peace is there when cement is set over a foundation of underlying hatred, remembered hurt and insult?

Peace! Can there be real peace when it is maintained with enforced occupation to oversee it?

Lord, of course I will continue to pray for 'justice and peace' for all mankind and forgive my faithless thoughts.

Let me only keep believing in your love and protection.

Let me only keep believing in the inherent good of the majority of peoples.

February 7th

My Mother's birthday.

Thank you Father for all the people who have had an influence on my life.

Lord I pray for the souls of all those I have loved who are now with you in eternal rest. I am ashamed and embarrassed that I ever took them for granted.

Help me to appreciate and treasure my family and friends who love and support me day by day.

Help me never again to be complacent in any relationship, however comfortable it may be.

February 8th

In the silence I
come to pray,
I come to meet my Lord.
I look into a candle flame
and whisper softly
Jesus' name
and know and feel Him here.

In the silence I
wait in faith
I wait to meet my Lord.
I think on all he means to me
and simply ask Him
'come to me'
and know and feel Him here.

In the silence I
surrender 'me'
to the service of my Lord.
I bow before his awesome power
and simply offer
every hour
of every day to Him.

February 9th

'Answers to everything you ever wanted to know!'

Well Lord, what a boast that is on the side of the cereal packet this morning, advertising an encyclopaedic DVD.

There is indeed much that I will never know. There is much I'm not bothered about knowing and other things about which I would love to be more informed.

However, where does that leave my faith? What is faith even?

I don't **know** you are there.

I don't **know** my prayers are heard.

But I do have faith, yes I can be convicted for it,

and so I **do** know

> that you are there and here with me every minute
>
> and that my prayers are heard
>
> and answered.

I don't need a DVD to inform me, I simply come to you in prayer, whenever, wherever I am, whatever I am doing and know, know with certainty, that you are there.

February 10th

Holy Spirit, sent by the Father, fill to overflowing those working to build your church in this place and remind us all that WE are your church.

Empower us to step out in praise of you and affirm in us the authority we carry when we call ourselves Christians.

As people of the New Testament help us to claim the promises given to us in the Gospel of Christ and, in that power, work to your praise and glory each in our own place.

February 11th

Holy and loving God, you said,

'My grace is all you need, for my power is strongest when you are weak.'

I feel weak just now with so many little niggles picking away at me, sapping my resolve not to worry, undermining my determination to keep things in perspective.

I am trying to juggle too many balls in the air as usual but am tired and so less able to cope.

I pray that your grace, which you give so freely and unconditionally, will be sufficient for me.

I pray that as I come to you, in expectation, I will be aware of your mercy through knowing your peace.

I pray for others who are bowed down at this time with situations beyond their control and fervently ask that they might receive the same loving support from their faith or the faith of others.

'I am most happy then to be proud of my weakness in order to feel the protection of Christ's power over me.'   2Cor.12.9

February 12th

Father of all, thank you for considering me worthy to serve you.

Thank you for the abundant grace which you pour onto me, which strengthens my faith and love in Christ Jesus.

Thank you that when I am beyond words, deep in self loathing for the way in which I constantly fail you, you are still there, loving and forgiving me.

Thank you that when I am faithlessly indecisive and constantly disappoint you, you are still there, loving me.

Thank you that your patience and forgiveness is beyond human understanding but free to all who seek you in their lives.

February 13th

Gosh it's cold today. The layer of frost on the blades of grass was so beautiful and I felt such an oaf trampling it down. Lord, walking the dog round the lake was like being in a wonderland with everything dredged in sugar crystals. It must be cold because she only went in the water once and then had the sense not to repeat the exercise and yet I know she loves the water, she can't pass a puddle without splashing through it.

Fancy the dog showing me the benefit of common sense.

How often do we carry on doing that which is really no good for us just because we like it?

How often do we cloak what was a pretty stupid idea in a respectable excuse?

Lord I pray that you will continue to show me the folly of my ways and help me to grow in wisdom, that in your loving and gentle way you will continue to hone me into a servant fit for the army of the King of Kings.

Thank you for this beautiful day.

February 14th

Saint Valentine's Day.

A day to celebrate love - a day to thank God for the very human emotion of love,

in all its guises,

in all its forms.

For the love of spouses and partners

for parents and children

for grandparents and grandchildren

sister to sister

brother to brother

for friends and neighbours

for pets and their owners

for colleagues and co-workers.

for the love of football supporters for their teams

for tennis fans and their stars

for pop fans and their idols.

For those working with love to bring Christian, Jew and Muslim closer together.

For those working with love to bring Hindu and Tamil closer together.

For those working with love, in whatever corner of the globe they operate.

Thank God for love.

Thank God for His Love.

February 15th

After all the celebration and prayerful rejoicing yesterday in celebration of love, I pray today for those who are lonely using words from Psalm 16

'You Lord are all I have,
And you give me all I need;
My future is in your hands.
How wonderful are your gifts to me;
How good they are.

You will show me the path that leads to life;
Your presence fills me with joy
and brings me pleasure for ever.'

February 16th

Lord I am taking today off. I am taking today just to be with you.

I am aware that I spend days squeezing my prayer time and quiet time into small spaces between other things.

How can I even hope to hear your voice if I keep breaking off for another appointment or phone call?

How can I hope to follow through a piece of your teaching if I never give you more than a few minutes here and there?

So Father as I drive off to my Quiet Day I ask for your safe keeping and pray that you will fill the time with your presence and that you will open my eyes to new possibilities and a greater understanding of you.

I pray that you will lead me, through prayer and meditation, to a place where I might be filled with the Holy Spirit and receive enlightenment in you, and I ask to return to the world empowered with new hope and 'new wine.'

Luke 5 :38

February 17th

That's life! What comes in with one hand is taken away by the other!

I had a truly special day yesterday Lord; a time of revelation and understanding, a time of total immersion, learning about the enormity of your power.

Today, back to earth, unpleasantness on every front, the news is awful in the media, I've already had a most unsatisfactory telephone conversation and the post arrived torn to shreds!

However, it's me who is at fault. I am annoyed at having to leave the perfection of yesterday to live in the real world of today. I actually begrudge having to get on with my life instead of staying in the safety of my retreat day, just dwelling on you and basking in your love for me. I am like a spoilt child not ready to leave the party and go home.

Lord please don't let me undo the good done during my time with you through my own petulance.

This is where you have planted me and this is where I must blossom and days of hot house pampering should only serve to make me bigger and stronger and lovelier, to reflect better your glory in the world.

Thank you for yesterday and thank you for today.

February 18th

Father of all who profess your name, who heard your knock and opened the door of their hearts,

    thank you for the strength of their faith.

Father of all whose faith is known only to you, who heard your knock and opened the door of their hearts,

    thank you for the strength of their faith.

Father of all those as yet unable to open the door more than a crack but who know you are there,

    thank you for their awareness.

Father of those still independent of you,

    may they soon hear

        and know

            and answer

                and enjoy, life in all its fullness.

February 19th

The constancy of the love of Christ for each one of us,

and the knowledge that each of one of us is met by our Lord at our point of need is truly wonderful and I meditate on the meaning of that for me today.

Jesus Christ is the same yesterday today and FOREVER!   Heb. 13 : 8

February 20th

Our Father in heaven,
hallowed be thy name,
sacred, holy,
sanctified, blessed
be thy name.

Father God thank you that through the life of your son here on earth we can approach your great and merciful throne, that we can make our supplications directly to you in all humility, accepting that we, of our own merit have no inherent right so to do.

The awe inspiring magnitude of what your son Jesus has enabled is beyond human comprehension and we accept that we will only ever know 'in part' until we can be with you in paradise. 1 Cor. 13:12

February 21st

Oh I do rejoice in the company of my friends Lord.

The fun and laughter we enjoy, the open and generous exchange of ideas, the sharing of family news, we are our own support network when one or other of us is a bit down.

I can't imagine how I would cope without them.

They are all different, their strengths and weaknesses meshed to make the strongest bond between us all. Some are close and I see them regularly, others are many miles away but we are in touch every few days by email. Some are once or twice a year correspondents and yet all of them Lord, each and everyone, I treasure and give thanks for.

They are your angels here in my daily life.

February 22nd

Holy Spirit who came to us through the flames of Pentecost, bringing the promise of power beyond human understanding, sweep through the mundane and mediocre management of peoples lives.

Lay flat the man made hierarchies of pomp and platitude, tarnish the self important idols of exploitation and greed and expose self-seeking hypocrisy paying lip service to concern and care.

Make compassion and a sincere desire to serve values to be lauded and appreciated.

Make modesty and humility features to be seen as strong not weak.

Turn the minds of those in positions of trust and power to the needs of the greater good.

Above all, give us who claim your promises, the conviction to take a stand when we feel your prompting, and not to always take the line of least resistance for the sake of a quiet life.

February 23rd

Jesus, you walked miles with your disciples and on unmade roads in sandals!

I want to give thanks for my feet today. I have been made aware of their very fundamental importance to my quality of life, and without their steadfast trustworthiness my daily round would be sadly compromised. I never think on the miracle of their construction or on the uses I put them to. Nor on the indignities I have put them through over the years as fashion has passed through various phases.

I never question their ability to cope as I set off to walk the dog or ride my bike or drive the car, or go round the supermarket or the farmers' market or walk to the pub on a lovely evening. The list is endless. And yet Lord they are just a rather fragile collection of bones, not much padding, wrapped in some skin.

Thank you for my feet and the health of them and I pray for those whose mobility is restricted by age or illness, whose feet are painful and more or less useless.

Lord show me where I could be more generous with my mobility in helping someone else.

February 24th

Where do you sit on the train?

Do you like to be near the front ready to make a quick get away at the station; or do you prefer to be a bit further back and take your time along the platform on arrival?

I have to say that for me it depends very much on where I am going. A meeting usually involves the graceless scrum with everyone else to the ticket barrier and out onto the pavement but a social day with a friend does not need to start with that urgency and I can meander more gently to the exit.

I wonder if there are parallels to be drawn with life.

There are those who will always need to be in the front carriage. They need to be as near the driver as possible, would be the driver if they could; the leaders, those up front dynamic people who need the cut and thrust, the high profile; they are the 'alpha' people.

Then there are those who sit a little further back towards the middle. Well balanced individuals who can roll with the punches, who because of their relative distance from the front can take a more objective view. They are bright and professional but not given to burn-out without just cause. These people can see both points of view and are often better because of it.

What about those who travel at the back of the train? Away from the danger of the engine, away from the phones and computers and tables full of important papers; are they any the less effective? Are they any the less capable? They really do take the time to digest information and draw very purposeful conclusions. They are the tortoise in the Tortoise and the Hare story. They will get there on time, even in plenty of time and they will have stopped to pick up a coffee on the way because they paced themselves.

Where do I sit on the train of life?

February 25th

Lord I take time today to meditate with praise on Psalm 36.verses 7-9

'How precious, O God is your constant love.
We find protection under the shadow of your wings.

We feast on the abundant food you provide;
you let us drink from the river of your goodness.

You are the source of all life and because of your light,
we see the light.'

Open my mind and my heart Lord to the promises in those words of David.

February 26th

Lord in yesterday's reading I realised that all the things needed for our survival; food, drink, shelter and light, are mentioned.

The basic factors with which to preserve life are promised to us through the words of the psalmists, prophets and disciples, time and again in the Bible.

That you should choose to use the allegory of these elemental items, as examples of what faith in you can bestow on us, is at once simple and yet immensely complex to absorb.

That you should want to provide for us and our bodily needs as a father is wonderful.

That we can access, through coming deeper into you, the very building blocks on which we can grow daily more Christ like is phenomenal.

Father grant in me the ability to grasp the truth of your teaching, and the application of it in my daily life.

February 27th

Dear God, what kind of a servant am I?

I didn't make time to come to you in a few minutes of quiet this morning.

I didn't offer myself in prayer to your service nor ask for your benediction on the day's comings and goings.

I didn't bring before you those who had asked me to pray for them.

I didn't give you a second thought.

Now here I am apologising for being

such a fair weather follower,

such a dilatory disciple,

such a pitiable pupil.

I am sorry.

February 28th

Feast day of St. Hedwig, 1399

Queen of Poland and model of faith; not one of the famous ones! She was the daughter of King Louis I of Hungary, ascending the throne at age thirteen. She married Jagiello of Lithuania only after he became a Christian, and then actively promoted Christianity in Lithuania.

Loving Lord, in whose arms the saints now rest, may we be inspired by the lives of these truly outstanding people. May we, through our knowledge of their lives, gain an insight into what being saintly really means. What their commitment to promoting the gospel of Jesus really cost them in terms of suffering, security and refuge. Then, perhaps we might think on the weak excuses we put before you in our intransigence and be humbled.

Leap Year Day

What will I do with this extra day Lord? How shall I spend this little bit of bounty? Shall I go and do something good and noble?

Shall I make an extra special effort to have some quality time with my family, some quality time in prayer and reading my bible?

Perhaps I could go shopping for something special, for me or for someone close to me.

Perhaps I could go to the cinema and meet friends.

Lord by the time I've thought about it I realise it's just another day. I'll do the things I do on any other day. Make the same hurried excuses for my omissions and the same lame excuses for my disaffection because of too many other commitments.

Then it will be the evening and bed time.

As I lay me down to sleep I pray the Lord my soul to keep.

March 1st

Saint David's Day.

Music and singing in Wales.

A land of great faithfulness and industry.

A land always ready to sing your praise.

A land peopled by souls who appreciate the beauty of the earth.

People who enjoy the rich bounty of your provision in their foods,

>from the earth agriculture and wonderful meat,

>from the sea lava for bread and fresh fish.

Loving Lord thank you for the great Christian teachers and leaders who have hailed from this fine country and for the ongoing outpouring of praise through the gifts you have given.

March 2nd

Noise, Noise, Noise

Everywhere I go someone is making noise!

So what? It shows I have my hearing, but Lord it is chaos.

Shopping; who decided there should be music to accompany my choice of breakfast cereals?

Walking to the shops I am assailed by oversized music systems in undersized cars as they thump passed me; heaven knows what it is like to travel in them.

Sitting on public transport next to someone with their head wired up to a personal music system – nothing personal about it.

Oh and Lord, the one way conversation over a mobile phone; even in the park, under the trees or on a bench in the sunshine, bird song being drowned out by

'she did' 'she didn't' 'she said' she didn't' babble babble babble!

I know I'll be a long time dead Lord but sometimes I want to scream for some silence.

March 3rd

Father it is me who must change my attitude.

'Cleanse the thoughts of my heart by the inspiration of your Holy Spirit'

'Take from my soul the strain and stress'

Comforting words which I say and sing so regularly.

Help me to accept the things which really shouldn't concern me in the first place.

Father God, on whose wisdom and goodness I should rely more fully, teach me, by the awareness of my shortcomings, just how liberating and life changing being committed to you can be. Ps 139:3-24.

March 4th

Lord, sometimes I am too muddled up to pray and yet I know for certain that you are here with me. I have so many things I want to ask you for, so many people for whom I want your loving guidance and protection.

And Lord I know that despite saying what I think you want to hear I have my own agenda which I would like sorting out. I know you know the thoughts of our hearts, so the weak mealy-mouthed offerings I make are a bit futile.

Knowing that you are here with me I come heavy of heart and mind, with no order of importance over those I'm thinking about, knowing that you will meet each and everyone of us at our point of need.

In that knowledge dear Lord I find rest, peace and confidence that tomorrow is another day.

March 5th

Today I had a long walk in the pouring rain and it was wonderful. I feel cleansed and invigorated and exercised and just so grateful to be alive.

I was dressed for the weather and so really enjoyed being out there watching the dog chase through the undergrowth, rudely scattering various little creatures from their shelters and birds from their dry perches.

I could tell that she was having a good time too, running freely on ahead to explore but coming back at regular intervals to touch base with me and make sure all was well. Then, if I hadn't seen her for a few minutes but could hear her crashing about I called her and she came running up expectantly, knowing that I would be pleased to see her and reward her with kind words of encouragement.

So many parallels with my life of faith Lord; the way you let me go off alone to live my life but knowing that I will check in regularly with you and that, in response to my answering your call, I will always be met with your loving kindness.

March 6th

Father forgive me for my opinionated outbursts, my vocalisation of self interest, the sweeping statements on topics about which I know very little.

Give me the courage to speak out when rational, well informed thoughts might be helpful but to know the limitations within which I do it.

'Do you my friend, pass judgement on others? You have no excuse, who ever you are. For when you judge others and then do the same as them you condemn yourself.
Rom.2:1-2

March 7th

Loving Lord, please help me today to be more ready to listen than to speak, to wait and hear through a situation before launching in like a gun going off 'half-cocked' with my opinion.

Father endow in me some wisdom

to know that the more knowledgeable,

the more thoughtful,

the more measured and considered,

the more sound

                   my eventual response might be.

March 8th

Creationist or Evolutionist? Have I got to be so dogmatically categorised?

I am reading a book about exciting new developments since the isolation and discovery of the human genome; that is, the complete set of human genes; 23 pairs of chromosomes, described in the book as:

'a record, written in 'genetish' of all the vicissitudes and inventions that characterised the history of our species and its ancestors since the very dawn of life' (Genome by Matt Ridley)

All I know for sure is that these bodies which we inhabit are the most amazing, the most awe inspiring pieces of processing apparatus. We exist with God and He in us. For those of us who have invited the Lord into our lives there is little argument outside of the rarefied world of academia. We might have evolved but we did it with the hand of divine guidance ever over the process. And, who but God himself could have overseen such an astonishing journey? We might have been created in the Garden of Eden but the end product is no less miraculous.

Whether our bodies are working well right now or less so, they are a Holy creation and I celebrate the life I have in mine; warts and all.

March 9th

No introspection today but an excess of happiness and over indulgence, celebrating a very special birthday with a very special friend.

Thank you for the feast days which punctuate our lives.

Thank you for the special people who scatter the moonshine of their personalities in our lives.

Thank you for the ability of the human spirit to respond to fun and laughter.

Thank you that we can get real enjoyment in sharing with others these attributes, drawing us into a closer fellowship with each other and building up the common good.

March 10th

If we were to base our faith in mankind on what the media feeds us we would give up on life and love and any hope of eternal peace; but Father we are surrounded by good if we stop and look.

By good neighbours and good friends.

By the smiles and the kindnesses of strangers.

By the welcome home from a much loved pet.

By the knowledge that our next meal is catered for.

By the knowledge that our homes are safe.

Father before we jump on the 'big bad world' band wagon may we stop and count our blessings.

Count your blessings count them one by one,

Count your blessings see what God has done,

Count your blessings,

Count them one by one,

And it will amaze you what the Lord has done.

                    Rev. Johnson Oatman, Jr.   Eph.1:3

Praise you Lord.

March 11th

I counted my blessing yesterday Lord and ended up feeling guilty because I have so much. From there I started to worry about guilt; when I don't think I have really done wrong and I remembered the teachings of a dear spiritual friend about good guilt and bad guilt. He maintained that bad guilt is a ploy of Satan's to undermine our faith; to enforce feelings of inadequacy, rejection or a need to be punished by God: in fact to make us doubt the sincerity of God's forgiveness and true grace.

God however has an answer.

'In love He predestined us to adoption as sons through Jesus Christ to Himself, according to the kind intention of His will, to the praise of the glory of His grace, which He freely bestowed on us in the Beloved. In Him we have redemption through His blood, the forgiveness of our trespasses, according to the riches of His grace, which He lavished upon us . . .' Eph. 1:4-8

Thank you for a conscience Lord but please give me the maturity to know when it is you prompting me and when I am in danger of being used unfairly.

March 12th

Lord from whom all goodness flows, from whom all compassion and patience emanate, lead me through the hours of today, tomorrow and this week. Show me the beauty of life lived through you and keep me in the ways of truth and honesty.

In Jesus name I pray.

March 13th

'Thine is the kingdom the power and the glory.'

Father in consecrating my life to you I became a child of the King of Heaven and a part of your Holy audience. That is really an amazing thing to think on, and I am not sure I can really understand the full impact of it. Maybe I never will whilst I am on earth.

Give me a thirst to know more of you through my prayers and give me a hunger to know more of you through reading my bible.

Keep me steadfast in my walk of faith, whatever the stumbling blocks along the way, and make me a fit child for your possession.

'For ever and ever, Amen'

March 14th

Gentle Lord I think of Psalm 119 and all the teaching contained within it, especially after yesterday's prayer.

Your word is a lamp to guide me and a light for my path.

I will keep my solemn promise to obey your instruction.   v's105-106

Father God accept my prayers and promises of a renewed spirit of faithfulness.

I ask in Jesus' name.

March 15th

Father I pray in the circular words of the old Celtic tradition today.

I pray that you will encircle me with your protection.

I pray that you will encircle those I love with your love.

I pray that in the circle of oneness with you I will find peace.

I pray that in the circle of oneness with you,
those for whom I pray will feel surrounded with care
and enveloped in peace.

March 16th

I'm cross about the cross
even though my salvation came from it.
I'm really cross about the cross
and the unspeakable agony it portrays.
I guess what makes me cross about the cross
is that I know, by my selfish
and thoughtless actions
I nail you back on it every day.
And I wear a cross around my neck,
a noose of love to remind me
that I must always be
cross about the cross
otherwise I wouldn't care
and you would still be hanging there
nailed by my indifference
in perpetual purgatory.
I'm glad I'm cross about the cross
because the evil of it needs
my anger to power me
with grateful acknowledgement,
to share its salvation.

March 17th

St Patrick's Day'

For all the saints we give thanks but Dear Lord was not this young man exemplary in his dedication and service to you?

I am surrounded by saints though; earthly, flesh and blood human beings with a divine capacity for selflessness and devotion to others.

Regular folk with whom I come into contact daily whose lives are a quiet example to me of commitment and faith.

Help me to find the saints in the here and now.

Help me to recognise them.

Make me more like them.

March 18th

A resurrection moment
A resurrection day
A punctuation in my walk of faith
which stops me short
and makes me say
He Lives!
A resurrection moment
A resurrection day
A knowing without any doubt
The Lord is here
and makes me say
He Lives!
And I must remember this moment of surety
And I must remember this day
And I must treasure this certainty against
the days when it's hard to say
He Lives!
When the lonely doubting moment
and the lonely doubting day
close over my head and suffocate my vision
obscure my thought away from heaven
but give me the faith Lord still to pray
He Lives!

March 19th

Lord the book I'm reading is sub titled 'Travels in a Betrayed Land' and at this time of year, focusing on your life's journey, I feel broken at the thought, that as your Holy Spirit travels through the time and space of this world, betrayed must be how you feel.

Betrayed at the greed and thoughtlessness of man to his brother.

Betrayed at the cruelty and corruption damming the lives

of the children whom you called to your knee.

Betrayed by hypocrisy and double standards in governments and ruling bodies.

Father I ask that we who profess you name and claim the faith of the Risen Lord will travel the world with you, will uphold, each in our own small sphere,

the teaching of a good and holy man;

will try to live by example through words and deeds, the goodness and mercy which came from your death.

We will affirm, we will proclaim, we will uphold, encourage, sustain and we will not simply rest in a betrayed land until the day of reckoning.

March 20th

I've been setting seeds today Lord in the expectation of a good harvest for the table, food for us to enjoy and hopefully a surplus to give away. It is always such a miracle that our plot, which looks so cold and barren just now, will be transformed over the coming months into a green, well ordered larder of goodness and vitality.

It would be trite to use these examples to illustrate the way your love and message can transform lives, which to all appearances are dead and barren, into fulfilled and productive engines of power.

But you can.

It would be an easy analogy to work with, seeds, barren land, fertile land, spiritual watering and food versus lack of nutrition and care.

But it is a fact.

It would be a simplistic and childish exercise to use such unsophisticated examples of your design for our lives.

But it is.

It is a simple fact that you can take a broken seemingly empty, seeming barren life, and make it whole;

and make it good,

and make it alive again,

and give it a full and productive reason to be.

March 21st

I thought today Lord about colour, there still isn't much about, it's very cold and grey, and not the sort of day for going out.

So I made a salad for lunch and the colours on the plate really made me think of the wonderful things there and the different tastes as I ate.

There was the red and happy tomato all shiny and full of good things, promising warmer days and an abundance of heavily draped vines in the greenhouse to look forward to.

The green crunchy lettuce leaves, roughly broken and drizzled with oil,

reminded me of holidays where aged trees heavy with hard little unripe fruit creak in the sun.

A hard boiled egg cut into slices making rings of pure white and revealing

the deepest golden middle, thank you hens.

Some chopped peppers making splashes of jewel bright radiance, like precious stones scattered in sunlight, capturing the transience of their beauty in a dancing prism.

It was such a simple bite of lunch Lord, or so I thought, but thanks to the dullness of the day I really saw it through new eyes and was taught a lesson.

For what I have just received make me truly thankful.

March 22nd

What does my carbon footprint say about the way I live my life?

Will the impression of my little size 5 make any difference at all to the global situation?

Is it not just a drop in the ocean compared to the polluting violence of superpowers?

Will the number of bins in my kitchen and the meticulous way in which I sort and segregate my rubbish really bring me carbon neutral status?

I am sorry for the total lack of respect certain sectors of the human race have for your world.

I am ashamed for the lack of regard with which we plunder the bounty provided for us.

I am embarrassed at the rape of the seas, the desecration of the forests, and the defilement of even the air you put above our heads.

Father I cannot undo the sacrilegious despoliation of our wonderful planet and I cannot really see how anything I can do is sufficient penance for ages of mismanagement but I will try. In the meantime let me not be so bowed down that my eyes become closed to the wonder and goodness around me.

Lord help me to begin to make only footprints that I am happy to have others walk in.

March 23rd

Glorious Lord,

Heavenly Father,

Supreme, omnipotent God,

Thank you for the sense of touch.

For the ability to feel the soft silky ears of my dog as she rests her head on my knee,

For the ability to feel the little fingers of a child grasp mine for safely and guidance,

For the ability to hold and hug and stroke and make a physical bond with someone through a hand patted, a heavy shoulder embraced, a worried forehead smoothed.

Glorious Lord in the silence of my prayers touch me.

March 24th

Mary, Mother of God, what hot tears of injustice you must have wept even though you knew your son was special. I often think of you when the cruelties which this world perpetrates on itself overwhelm me. I never think of you laughing and enjoying your family, only ever full of grief at the foot of the cross.

Father teach me how to cope in proportion to my situation.

Father teach me how to react in appropriate measure to my situation.

Father teach me the value of a mountain and a mole hill and give me the power to discern one from the other.

Father show me when it is right to cry and gnash my teeth and when it is more effective to clothe myself in the joy which knowledge of you brings and to greet the world with gladness.

March 25th

'2 for the price of 1'
'3 for 2'
'Buy now Pay Later'
'12 Months free credit'
Loyalty points, Favoured Customer Rates, Air Miles.

What a good customer can expect today.

What do I get for signing up to you Lord?

The peace of the Lord Jesus Christ,
The absolute knowledge that I am never alone,
The love of someone who will never let me go,
The promise of eternal life.

That's an offer I would be mad to ignore.

March 26th

What joy in a cup of coffee with friends, sharing anecdotes about children, husbands, grandchildren.

One tale sparking remembrance in another.

One story bringing joy and fun to the rest of us.

One soul mate willing to open up a treasure trove of memory for the rest of us to enjoy.

Laughter is a tonic and the benefits of it don't really need scientific affirmation.

We glowed with collective health as we went our separate ways.

March 27th

Today has been so lovely. Unseasonably warm, a mercurial change after the last couple of weeks, in fact warm enough to be outside without a sweater. Can you believe it, in March!

Of course you can believe it! What am I saying?

I loved it. I did some gardening and tidied up the shed. I took the dog for an extra walk and noticed all sort of spring flowers, flies and bugs as I went through the fields and by the river.

So here is my dilemma, on days like today I appreciate the climate change which makes it possible to be outside, to have a shorter winter, to feel my cells respond to the rays of the sun on my body.

March 28th

'Father hear the prayer I offer, not for ease that prayer might be'

-but Lord that I might through quiet contemplation today, learn more of your will for me.

As I sit in silence with the words of that hymn fresh in my mind I ask that you will

'Be my strength in hours of weakness,
in my wanderings be my Guide;
through endeavour, failure, danger,
Saviour, be thou at my side.'

Love Maria Willis, 1864

March 29th

Bombs in cars and scars of war,
innocent victims caught up in battles
for supremacy.
Men who are right with sight of salvation,
bigots, fanatics inflicting deep wounds
for supremacy.
Chaos and shouts in bouts of terror,
innocent victims caught up in battles
for supremacy.
Prayers of peace from priest and imam,
faithful pilgrims bowed down in prayers
for unity.

March 30th

Lord look with grace on the people
across on the other side of the world who
pick tea and harvest coffee.
I wish they could know how much we appreciate
the comfort and refreshment which these two,
once so precious, now so common, drinks bring.
I wish they could know how many sad tear stained faces
are slowly and gently turned around
over a mug of coffee,
how many situations are put back into context
over a cup of tea.
Whether instant or freshly ground, tea bag or
select blending, thank you to them and
I pray that the exploitation which they have suffered over
the years is now being more honourably addressed.

March 31st

'The Revelations of Divine Love'

Even the words of this title are immensely powerful. A revelation by implication is something that someone wants either to show or to have discovered: that being so, then the Lord was indeed very present when he came so clearly to Julian of Norwich.

Divine, by the connotations we put upon the word today is heavenly, gorgeous, more than special, the exact opposite of earthly. So, Divine Love? Just a huge way of saying something more than any mere human can begin to comprehend.

Whatever we have experienced in our lives which we attribute to the emotion 'love' can only be a glimpse of the real thing when measured next to the 'divine love' of our Heavenly Father.

Gracious Lord, thank you that through the extreme dedication and sacrifice of those who heard your call in earlier times, we can still learn more of you and grow in that knowledge to receive more of your love for us.

April 1st

Lord I am still thinking about the title of Mother Julian's writing from yesterday. Another interpretation of the word 'divine' is to discover, to deduce, to discern, and to perceive.

And I am learning through her writing, I am discovering, I am perceiving the greater message about servant-ship which I pray will bring me closer to knowing more of you.

So the revelations which you gave to this wonderful mystic are still here to be explored and learned from and they are as accessible and appropriate to the new millennium as they were in 1373.

May I continue to divine your meaning and purpose for me each day.

April 2nd

'The Lords Courtesy', another of Mother Julian's 'shewings'. Father forgive me, not so much for what I do or don't do with people day by day, though that is important, but for the lack of courtesy I show to you. I am ashamed by the lack of civility with which I throw prayer at you, the lack of consideration and politeness with which I rush into my pew before a service, having caught up with everyone else first.

God of the Divine Revelations keep faith with me and I will try to learn from those whose words are your tender directions and I will, with your help realise the meaning of your Divine Love.

April 3rd

I accepted an offer of help today and I saw the joy on the face of the person I'd asked. Forgive us our stubbornness in trying to always manage, in trying to be all things to all people and in so doing neglecting our own needs.

We are always so ready to offer help but very poor at asking for it and when I recognised the pleasure my Good Samaritan friend had in helping me I was humbled and happy at the same time.

Lord help me to ask and then receive with grateful thanks.

April 4th

Talking of quiet gratitude Lord, I want to pray today for all the young folk in our communities. I am so saddened by the bad press they get. There will always be the rotten apples in the barrel but we have such a lot of decent, honest, fun loving youngsters around. Lord give me the words to intercede on their behalf when I hear blanket accusations flying around, give me the discernment to know how best to speak up on their behalf and more importantly help me never to pre-judge groups of young folk myself as I go by them, when I'm out. These are our future leaders, carers and parents and we should be encouraging them into maturity not crushing them into categories of suspicion and doubt.

April 5th

'Whatever happens let your conduct be worthy of the gospel of Christ…..stand firm, united in spirit and in mind…' Phil.1-27

Heavenly Father how often I am aware, only with hind sight, that I have not fulfilled my promise and that I have let you down with a careless or thoughtless word. How often I don't stand firm, but let myself be blown by the winds of circumstance. An invitation to go out for the day so readily accepted when I had thought I would spend it in prayerful study of your word or making a visit to a neighbour less able to get out and about.

How apposite is the Letter of Paul to the Philippians – even today!

April 6th

Oh Lord what a great walk with the dog this morning, and with my friend and her dog. We have prayed our way through the woods, lifting those of our community to you in grateful supplication; knowing that you hear and see and know all our doings almost before we do. We have brought our families before you and then, in a clearing we sat together in quiet, companionable silence and closed our eyes. We just stayed still knowing we were in your presence. We opened our hands and arms to embrace the love of God in the warmth of the sun. We turned our faces upward to feel the soft breeze, like a celestial kiss, brush across our cheeks.

What a privilege it all was and what an affirmation of our faith.

April 7th

I have been thinking about the superlative laden dialogue we are bombarded with today. It is absolutely incredible that such a cataclysmic, catastrophic, miraculous, phenomenal, extraordinarily, unbelievable book like the bible should be a best seller. With little words like great, joy, love, accept, kingdom, birth, salvation, building into stories of compassion; bringing to life examples of faith and fulfilment then, all written and translated into understandable short verses which have changed lives. Now that is truly remarkable.

No hyperbole, no verbosity, just succinct writing which honours and serves the greatness of the script.

The story of our Lord Jesus is so wonderful; I think if it were written in today's dialogue we would have expired from our own exaggeration way before the resurrection.

April 8th

Father in heaven, Father who wants me to endeavour to walk in the footsteps of Jesus day by day; show me how.

Show me how to walk in faithful submission to your will,
despite my chuntering and grumbling about other things as I do.

Show me how to listen and perceive your purpose for me
in spite of my rebellious and disobedient nature.

Give me an understanding of your omnipotence, which makes the care you have for me so bottomless, even though I don't deserve it.

I want to walk in the footsteps of Jesus every day, unconditionally.
I want to give everything I do into your keeping, unconditionally.
Help me to grow more devoted to serving you as you may lead me, unconditionally.

April 9th

The Bible is the big black book
with which we clout ganglions out of existence.

The Bible is the big black book
with which we add extra inches to the end of the bed
to help blood pressure.

The Bible is the big black book
with names and dates going back generations inside the front pages.

The Bible is the big black book
holding all the history of my family from Abraham and Isaac to the Apostles and Jesus:
Oh, and God,
my Father.

What an amazing book The Holy Bible is.

April 10th

'In memory of James Peabody, a true friend'

This is carved on a bench by the path on one of the walks I take.

Lord, what will people say of me? How will people remember me?

In the final analysis it is only your opinion of me that matters but please, help me to live in such a way that I can be called

'a true friend'.

April 11th

The Lord was an angry god when he gave Jeremiah the holy messages to relay.

Not fearing for his own safety he told the people; he delivered the unpalatable truth; he made no wishy-washy précis of the Lord's words but with due reverence delivered the dire warnings.

Fire and famine, war and want would be upon those who denied their Lord, who lived immoral lives, who stole, who spoke ill of another, who worshipped idols; each generation more wicked and wilful than the last carrying on their own sweet way.

We too Lord in this new millennium, surrounded by war and want, famine and flood, should surely be drawing some parallels and learning, albeit from three thousand years ago, the message which Jeremiah died trying to bring to his people.

Father give all who profess your name an ounce of the passion of Jeremiah and great things will be done on this planet in your name.

April 12th

It is good to remember the angry God of the Old Testament. It is all too easy in these days of relative comfort for a vast proportion of us to pay lip service to God. There is a chummy, pally sort of relationship offered, an accessibility, which is in danger of undermining and demeaning the awesomeness of our Heavenly Father.

As much as The Trinity is separate yet whole, we find rather more comfort in being around Jesus the son, and whilst knowing he has a strict father, we try not to come up against him too often.

Father God, made recognisable and approachable through your son our Saviour Jesus, forgive us when we lack the reverence and respect your presence in our lives demands.

April 13th

Lord thank you for diversions. No two days are the same. I have spent the last hour away from my desk chasing escaped chickens back into their run. I can quite see how the tender green shoots of all my spring plantings would be far more attractive than a boring old pen of earth but that's life if you are a chicken! They are funny and they do make me laugh. I'm sure they have a whole philosophy of their own; if only I could tap into it perhaps my complicated days and ways would be more predictable and less frenetic.

The joy of fresh eggs every day never palls and the feeling of immense gratefulness to them for their clever bounty is everlasting.

So, sorry you couldn't have a couple of hours to gorge yourselves in my new salad bed ladies, sorry you couldn't fill up on the juicy green pea and bean shoots, but you will get some eventually even if only as leftovers from a good dinner table.

April 14th

I was a little annoyed yesterday at having to stop what I was doing to rescue the hens, or rather rescue my kitchen garden from the hens. I'm sure it wasn't the Lord's will that they got out but with His loving bias put on the situation I was able to appreciate the break I took, the exercise I had and certainly the comic faces of the birds, as they resigned themselves to their re-incarceration; it was a tonic.

Thank you Lord for perspective and help me to look for it more often.

April 15th

'All things bright and beautiful' - what a lovely hymn that was during schooldays. There is a lot of inspired and very spiritual new hymn writing going on Lord and certainly with words that have more resonance for the multi faceted lives people live today, but wait…….

Looking at the words of our children's hymns with adult eyes I see words of wisdom for all ages and times.

'Tell me the stories of Jesus, I love to hear' and still do.

'Jesus wants me for sunbeam' well I guess there isn't an age limit on being a sunbeam is there?

'Jesus loves me this I know' and how important has that knowledge been.

'I will make you fishers of men' – have I been?

Father God, thank you for those who continue to write words and music in praise of you. Thank you also for those whose inspiration in the past still brings comfort and sustenance to millions around the globe.

April 16th

Praise the Lord, all nations extol him,
All you peoples;
For his love protecting us is strong,
The Lord's faithfulness is everlasting. Praise the Lord.

Ps 117

It hard to think that the words of David have any relevance to today when the news is full of pictures and stories from around the world of war and factions ripping into each other in the name of religion.

Father God help me to hold faith and accept that you have the ultimate power in spite of how little sense I can make of things.

April 17th

Oh Lord, I do give the benefit of my opinion too readily.

Then I remember:

'Do not judge and you will not be judged. For as you judge others so will you yourself be judged'.

Matt.7 1-2

Forgive me for being so quick to set myself up as the arbiter of right or wrong.

Forgive me for being expert witness and evaluator, critic and jury.

Help me to still my tongue and redirect my thoughts to consider your view of a situation.

Help me remember the words of Matthew more often.

Father hear my prayer and move in my heart to bring about change.

April 18th

Lord what good are all these sound bites and instant texts? How can people make a rational decision about anything when an instant response is constantly called for? How can crucial actions be instigated on a nano seconds thought?

What a lesson we learn through faith when we acknowledge 'your time not mine.'

What a lesson we learn through faith when we submit to your will and your schedule.

What a lesson we learn through faith when we submit to your greater plan.

What peace in our hearts when we wait on you in the silence.

April 19th

Father, how do I pray for situations which are far beyond my control?

How do I pray for situations on which I can have no influence of affect whatsoever?

I bring them to you for your deliberation.

I will hold them up until my arms loose their blood and become numb,

but is that what you want?

How can I meet the magnitude of a situation by sitting quietly and just handing the burden over to you?

It seems such a cop-out to say

'I can't handle this Lord so I'm giving it to you to sort out.'

Should I prostrate myself on the floor to show my submission to your will?

Is fasting and prayer the way to prove my sincerity to you?

Do I need to prove my sincerity to you? You can see what's in my heart.

Should I keep praying or does that make me a pestering child?

Would I be wiser to bring my problems and worries to you,

lay them reverently before you and then walk away, in faith,

knowing you will have heard and seen and will take the appropriate action?

What is 'appropriate action'? Is it what I add in the caveats I attach to my prayers? the unspoken thoughts, but very much a part of my supplication, on the way I would like things to turn out.

Lord give me the faith of a child, the trust of a child and the pure, honest sincerity of a child.

Lord help me to pray in simple, uncluttered, unaffected faith, knowing that that is all I need do.

April 20th

A glorious spring day.

A glorious, outsized, sunny spring day.

Thank you for such a blessing, for such a polished, new day.

I want to clean the windows of my soul to receive more of this divine goodness.

I want to clean the clouds from my eyes to appreciate and take in the illuminated beauty of everyday things.

Dew resting on leaves, diamonds to stop me in my tracks.

Cobwebs moving sinuously in a gentle motion, beckoning me to notice them.

A blackbird calling out to his love across the lawn.

A robin telling the cat off for walking across the grass.

A glorious spring day.

A glorious, outsized, sunny spring day.

Thank you God.

April 21st

What have we in common with other faiths Lord?

Help me to learn more of our similarities and the things on which we might build.

Help me to look for the positive, wholesome philosophies we share rather than negative differences which divide and breed suspicion.

Thank you for diversity, for the mixture, for the assortment of races and creeds with whom we live and work.

May this theological miscellany encourage us all to think more about our own relationship with God and what we might do to deepen our own convictions and faith.

It is surely in a meeting of minds and deeper understanding that we can bring peaceful harmony to our communities.

April 22nd

'Isn't she doing well?', 'isn't he being brave?', 'aren't they amazing?'

Father how many time do we recognise someone's hurt with these empty acknowledgements.

'I bet she wants to scream', 'I imagine he wants to punch something', 'I think they would like to shout and lash out',

No, we wouldn't say those things but do we give those, whose hurt is beyond our reach, the space to do it? To get angry, to rail against the world and you too Lord if they need to. Do we give them room to uncover their wounds to the air, or do we prefer it if they behave with dignity and keep everything wrapped up?

Give me the sensitivity to help with another's pain.

Give me loving arms of patience and strength to hold them whilst they fight.

Give me gentle silence to absorb their angry words.

Give me discernment to tend raw, exposed hurt with the salve of your redeeming love.

April 23rd
St George's Day

The cult of St George probably first reached the kingdom of England when the crusaders returned from the Holy Land in the 12th century. King Edward of England was known for promoting the codes of knighthood and in 1348 founded the Order of the Garter. During his reign, George came to be recognised as the Patron Saint of England.

In 1969, St George's Feast day was reduced to an optional memorial in the Roman Catholic calendar; the solemnity of his commemoration depends on purely local observance. He is, however, still honoured as a saint of major importance by the Eastern Orthodox Church.

'Reduced to an optional memorial' how readily we play God today; how readily we disparage the achievements of bygone ages as having less relevance to life now than then.

Lord in these disseminated times, where new values and meaning are being attached to our institutions; help us to remember and respect those whose story has been a fundamental part of our history. For the greater good or the greater shame Lord teach us by their examples and help us to learn from them.

April 24th

Magnitude, what a wonderful word! It uses all the parts of my mouth to say it.

It can't be said without a complimentary expression on my face.

Magnitude, enormous, colossal, I feel the power of the words.

The Love of God for each and every one if us is even bigger than that!

Praise the Lord!!

April 25th

'If we really want to pray, we must first listen, because it is in the silence that God speaks.'

I don't know to whom these words should be attributed but I dwell upon them in silence of today.

April 26th

Dear Lord, if I am to hear you and know you and be more attentive to you I must draw away from the everyday.

I must go to a place of quiet.

A place where I know there will be no telephone, no text message, no email; nothing in fact to break the space between us.

I can't take myself into the desert as Jacob and Moses did, I can't get very far away from civilisation at all.

Where can I go to devote all my being to you in this busy busy world?

I will go to church.

I will walk in the church yard, absorbing the peace and tranquillity, the majesty and the ageless gentle, gracious love which seeps out of the stones.

I will sit in communion amongst the memorials to faithful souls who now bask in your radiance.

I will sit surrounded by symbols of your glory and breathtaking promise.

I will wait on you with an open heart in my own sacred space.

In the desert where my thirst for you rages show me that I am never deserted.

April 27th

A dear friend is having real problems with her neighbours Lord. I know there are two sides to every story but I cannot imagine that she and her family could have done anything to merit such unjust treatment and open hostility. It would be easy to draw all sorts of comparisons from this and build the picture into an analogy for the wider community, the local district, the national or international scene, but I won't.

I ask simply that there might, between them, be found some similarity, some common ground on which they may start to build an amicable status quo.

I am wondering however, if there is anyone that I personally should be trying harder with.

Gracious Lord Help me not to be so wrapped up in everyone else's problems that I don't see properly for the plank in my own eye.

April 28th

It said on the weather forecast this morning that it was foggy in Scotland.

Here in East Anglia it is gin clear and bright; I'm glad I'm here and not there.

I wonder though, in all this clarity, am I in danger of seeing less, of knowing less? Perhaps with vision misted I would be forced to look more deeply, have patience to wait for my eyes to acclimatise to the poor visibility.

Perhaps in the clouded world of today's Scottish landscape I would find an inner enrichment which would bring clarity, which would enable a more profound interpretation, which would bless me with a more insightful understanding of God's purpose for me.

April 29th

Well Lord thank you for another lovely day. I have opened all the windows and a gentle breeze is blowing through the house, taking out the stale winter atmosphere and bringing in clean, sweet, spring air.

My study window is as wide as it will go and I feel as though great pillows of heaven are being fluffed up around me.

It feels good.

I feel good.

Thank you Father.

April 30th

'Why?' I asked the caller on the phone, 'why do you need my date of birth?'

I wasn't very gracious, in fact I was rather short and he was only doing his job. He was trained to collect and collate information for someone else to make capital out of, but it wasn't his personal fault.

I resent being tracked, traced and monitored by invisible corporations. I feel it an intrusion and violation of my personal space, my human rights even….and when did we get those Lord?

On the one hand we are battling for a fairer world for everybody, equality in all aspects of life and love and on the other hand we are more enslaved than ever to bodies for which we hold no particular allegiance.

I wish I could make sense of it.

You are the only one who knows my 'goings out and comings in'.

Ps 121 : 8

You are the only one who knows more about me than I do about myself and I am comfortable and at peace with that.

I am sorry I was short with the young man on the phone though.

May 1ˢᵗ

'Mayday' a day of traditional springtime celebrations pre-Christianity associated with fertility rites; new life, new crops, fecundity.

'Mayday' 1889 designated Labour Day, a day to celebrate work and the right to work under acceptable conditions.

'Mayday' an international distress signal.

'Mayday' in the new millennium, a bank holiday, a time for families to be together, of socialising with friends, of spring cleaning or decorating, often the first BBQ of the season.

Mayday, another day to be put to good use.

May 2ⁿᵈ

The words of this song by The Kinks should be sung by Christians every day.

Thank you for the days,
Those endless days, those sacred days you gave me.
I'm thinking of the days,
I won't forget a single day, believe me.

I bless the light,
I bless the light that lights on you believe me.
And though you're gone,
You're with me every single day, believe me.

Days I'll remember all my life,
Days when you can't see wrong from right.
You took my life,
But then I knew that very soon you'd leave me,
But its all right,
Now I'm not frightened of this world, believe me.

Amen.

DAYS words and Music by Ray Davies©1968 Davray Music Ltd & Carlin Music Corp. All Rights Reserved and used by permission.

May 3rd

'There is no time in touch'

I have just read that phrase and it moved me.

How rich or poor we are, how old or young,
how feeble or strong; a touch is empowering.
A touch sanctions, a touch endorses.
A touch makes language seem impoverished.

Wisdom in the touch of the elderly,
trust in the touch of a child,
healing in the touch of compassion,
benediction in the touch of prayer.

Lord God, in whose hands was so much healing and power, give me the grace to impart your love through a touch.

May 4th

Lord having you in my day gives even the wettest flagstone beauty.

Of course I could appreciate and marvel at the colours released by the water if I were not a Christian.

Of course I could still wonder at the geological process which brought such a lovely piece of stone into being.

Of course I could still be grateful to the stonemason for using his skill to cut and fashion the flag.

It is lovely though and I am pleased to have someone with whom I can share it right now and to whom I can say thank you.

May 5th

'Trust in the Lord with all your heart and lean not on your own understanding.' Prov. 3-5

So when we pray for guidance and clarity to cope with a situation, or to make an informed decision, at work or home; let us remember the last few words.

'lean not on your own understanding.'

Father I readily offer a problem or potential worry up to you, but then, so quickly begin to add the pertinent factors as I see them.

Help me not to 'lean on my own understanding' which is so often flawed or biased, but to wait on you for clarification and direction.

May 6th

Lord, I should, in the light of yesterday's prayer, think today on Psalm 31 verses 3-5

You are my rock and my stronghold; for the sake of your name
 lead and guide me.
Set me free from the net that has been set to catch me, for you
are my refuge.
Into your hands I commit my spirit and you deliver me,
 Lord, you God of truth.   Amen.

May 7th

I shared a particularly lovely bottle of wine last night with friends. We appreciated everything about it. The wonderful deep red, almost black colour, the complex scent, the way is seemed to grow in flavour as we held it in our mouths, so many senses to be awakened.

This morning as I thought about our lovely evening, saluting the vineyard and vintner, I was suddenly consumed by an awareness of all the lives that are ruined by drink; the fractured families, the broken homes; and the joy of a special time was tarnished.

I am sorry for those whose lives are a complicated battle with addictions but I am angry that I should somehow feel guilty for enjoying something which to them spells disaster.

Am I over sensitive Lord?

Is my conscience going into free fall unnecessarily?

Lord, help me to know the difference between awareness and guilt and to be able to work within the meaning and expectations of them.

May 8th

Fat free, sugar free, low salt,

half fat, low-cal, cordial light,

easy spread, long life.

Father is it any wonder with all this watering down, letting down, supplementing, replacing that we can't digest the real thing anymore?

Preserve me from diluting your message; from making it so accessible that I erase the meaning from the words.

Help me to keep the significance and worth of Jesus in my conversations.

Help me to relay the enormity of the message, the worth of the message.

Help me to relate your glory in all its full, undiluted strength.

May 9th

Silent old stones
towering into ageless
celebrations of confidence
for what you represent.
Warm old stones
mothering arms wrapped
round centuries of
children at prayer.
Hard old stones
scarred but still solid
protecting those who
seek your safety.
Singing old stones
playing back the tunes of ages voices
praising God in styles
and costumes varied.
Miraculous old stones
celebrating the bones
that carved you, built you,
loved you, visited you,
brought young to you, lovers to you,
dead to you and
from where they received benediction.

May 10th

Father I pray for all religious leaders today. Grant them quiet patience and strength, the culmination of years of practice, to work together for an understanding of each others theologies. Not that we should have to be in subjection to a faith to which we can't or don't subscribe, but in order that the ultimate consensus reached might be one of acceptance and respect.

Lord direct their discourse and understanding, enhance their generosity each to the other and bring about a sacred regard on which the future peace of nations might grow.

May 11th

Tulips, lots of them, all shapes and colours, planted in clumps to make a vibrant, showy splash.

Tall thin ones with spiked tips to the petals, little fat ones with green stripes up the petals.

Big blowsy parrot tulips with huge raggedy heads and the Renaissance man's friend 'The Rembrandt', in my opinion one of the most wonderful.

Colour from white and lemon through reds and oranges to the Black Knight, actually deepest purple.

Glorious ice cream sundae bowls of the pink and white Angelique and all at different heights so that each one can have its own place in the curtain call of spring splendour.

Thank you for these beautiful bulbs.

Thank you for the local parks where we can enjoy such breathtaking profusion.

May 12th

The fragility of life was borne out on the news today with another young life snuffed out in a car crash. Our roads here in the fens are long and straight and in some parts quite narrow. They are sufficient for everyday purposes but there isn't much room to manoeuvre in case of a misjudged movement whilst driving. The dykes on one or both sides are steep, the water is deep, and a car entering at speed invariably goes in nose first: but, if you are wont to, you can drive very fast for several miles.

So, for a moment's lack of concentration another young man has lost his life, another family is plunged into mourning. It happens so often that the headline is just another statistic.

How shocking is that admission?

Dear Father, whose hurt in seeing precious lives wasted is never dulled, is never diminished, and for whom every soul is perfect and special; teach me how to cope with and react to situations in which I have no apparent involvement. Accept my prayers for the soul of the young man and may those who are left, with only their memories, feel a blanket of prayer being wrapped around them.

May 13th

When heaven seems far away, when I feel so very distant from the child of God I'm supposed to be, I close my eyes and picture Jacobs's ladder. I see the golden structure stretching up into the clouds, lined with angels from the realms of glory. Then I am reminded that there is a permanent pathway to heaven bought and paid for with the life of Jesus. And I thank God for his gift of salvation which restores my soul and brings me back to the way of truth.

May 14th

I have just taken a phone call from someone ringing to see how I was. They hadn't seen me around for a while, our paths hadn't crossed in the usual places and so he called. I am very touched. I never think that I would be missed if I weren't to turn up at one of my customary venues. How dreadful is that? I who love my friends to bits, who would do anything for them, have never considered that they too might be capable of that measure of love reciprocally? It isn't that I have deliberately dismissed their valuation of my friendship, just that I haven't really thought about it until now.

Father please forgive my stupidity and complete lack of understanding of 'koinonia' and accept my thankfulness and appreciation of all those whose fellowship enriches my life.

May 15th

'Give Him the glory.'

What a simple little phrase. We say it and sing it so often yet the magnitude of that command is phenomenal.

'Give Him
 the magnificence
       the splendour
              the beauty
                     the wonder
                            the grandeur
                                 the brilliance
                                     the credit
                               the fame
                         the praise
                   the laurels
             the triumph
      the admiration
the stardom.

Give Him the glory? Oh yes Lord; and then some!

May 16th

'and forgive us our trespasses, as we forgive those who trespass against us'

But do I? Am I always able to administer the same fairness to those who might have in some way hurt or slighted me as I expect from my Father in heaven?

I don't think so.

I don't have His almighty power.

I don't have his almighty benevolence.

There should be large warning light flashing as I realise this fact;

that I will receive from Him only in measure to that which I serve out.

Father, help me not to draw a cloak of wounded feeling around me for warmth but rather throw it off as contaminated and release with grace those against whom I hold a grudge.

May 17th

Dear Heavenly Father, in whose hands everything conceivable is held, meet me at my point of need I pray.

Meet me on the wordless path of confusion where I stand marooned and feeling small.

Meet me in the fog of unknowing where I fear to move.

Meet me in the sea of souls where the cries of the lost are deafening.

Father God, lift me from these places back into the light of certainty and assurance.

Father God lift me back into the safety of your arms.

May 18th

Angels. Angels are everywhere. They are in the hearts and minds of lovers flushed with each new discovery of their similarities and differences. They are in the songs they sing to each other.

Angels are in our hymns, aiding our words and tunes to ascend into the highest high, to the throne of God.

We seek their protection and guidance as we sleep or for our loved ones as they journey.

They are on cards for new born babies and the gravestones of the deceased.

We speak of guardian angels.

They are heavenly, divine, godly beings from whom we gain great comfort and with whom we feel we can have a relationship.

I don't know with certainty that they are as readily accessible as we might wish.

I do know that they exist though and that they are here on earth with us.

Every day, as kindnesses are done, as thoughtful acts and joyous giving, from one human being to another are carried out, I know angels exist.

May 19th

What posture do you adopt when you pray?

Does it show a lack of respect if we don't prostrate ourselves as the medievalists thought appropriate?

Should we kneel upright on flag stones whilst beating ourselves in penitence?

Is there a prescribed way in which we should come before the throne of God?

What did Jesus do?

Sometime he sat, sometimes he stood, once he did prostrate himself, sometimes he had his hands raised in blessing. More often than not he was looking heavenward. Matt.26-39

Lord there are days when I pray standing on the train, walking the dog or gardening.

Lord there are days when I come in deep respect on my knees in a posture of submission to your will.

There are times when I pray as lie down to sleep or as I sit in the chair looking out at nothing particular.

Whatever posture I adopt, my faith in a Listening God is immutable.

Whatever posture I adopt I never forget that I am going into the Holy of Holies.

Whatever posture I adopt my heart beats in adoration of my Lord.

May 20th

Irritation and compassion are such extremes of emotion and yet I feel them both so many times a day. Loving Lord Jesus what sort of a person am I who can so easily switch from one to the other? How can I snap at one situation and cry at another, seconds apart?

I only know that you are with me and support me, gently chastising my irascibility and smiling down on my compassion.

I ask that I might know when it is appropriate to be angry and to be able to use my anger for good purposes.

I ask that I might know the difference between compassion and useless, self mortification.

Father, I pray that the refining fire of the Holy Spirit might cleanse the darker corners of my personality and strengthen the weaker ones.

May 21st

'No one lights a lamp and then puts it under a bowl.

Luke 8-16

I wonder how many of us are so busy trying to be humble and gracious that we completely diminish our God given talents. How many of us, in trying to be modest actually cover, without trace, the glory of the Lord's hand in our makeup? I know there are times when I frustratedly take a back seat for fear of seeming to be blowing my own trumpet but where I know I could be of value: times when I don't put myself forward for fear of being thought a busy-body or know-all.

Lord help me to feel the power of your spirit encouraging and endorsing me when I sit at the crossroads of indecision and forgive me for the times when I have hidden the evidence of your hand on my life through cowardice or misplaced reticence.

May 22nd

I have been asked to give a testimony about a colleague at a farewell party.

I can do that. I have indication and proof of my observations.

I have evidence and can give witness to demonstrate and support my opinion.

My statement will be a 'declaration, an authentication, an acknowledgement' of all the attributes of the much loved character about whom I will speak.
def Testimony OED

I have often heard people in church meetings asked to give their testimony.

Based on the above list of determining factors to define, etymologically, the word testimony, one can understand why they are usually so overwhelmingly compelling.

Whilst it is less easy to have indications of proof and evidence; or supported, authenticated examples of the effect of the spirit on a person's life, there is none the less an overwhelming and indisputable response to it: a life changing power which has physical and spiritual manifestations.

I ought to think more about the meaning of 'testimony' with relation to my own faith.

May 23rd

The vegetable beds are beginning to spill over the path and I look with wonder, as I do each year, at the sight. I'll take a bowl of mixed salad leaves in for supper, and a few new potatoes which, apart from a wipe with a cloth don't need washing. There are some baby carrot thinnings, not a feast but a taste, a promise of things to come. There are some broad beans too which only I like, so I will have them as I enjoy them best, barely cooked and tossed in a drop of olive oil.

A glass of elderflower cordial, made last spring and I will feel like a lord at my own banquet.

I will raise my glass to the 'unseen guest' and say thank you, a warm, grateful thank you.

May 24th

A light, fresh, sunny morning and I decided that a good walk was in order. The dog was particularly impressed, I think she had become resigned to very inferior perambulations round the nearest, smallest field. Her good natured acceptance of whatever comes her way is truly exemplary and her biddable character, whether in a feast or famine of exercise, is enviable. Her equilibrium is only ever upset if food is late but then, since she has a better internal time clock than Greenwich, I know when 5pm and supper time is imminent because a large black head comes to rest on my knee.

I know she doesn't have deadlines to meet or a mortgage to pay but there is a lot to be learnt from the day to day existence of a black Labrador.

May 25th

I come to the fountainhead, the wellspring, the source of my life and I stand in the cascade. I stand and receive all that there is to take from the origins of time and space and I am enriched, energised and bursting with goodness. Bursting with the goodness of the Lord and I know, that whatever this day has for me, I will be supported and mightily sustained.

'Do you trust and believe?'

Oh yes, I trust and believe.

May 26th

'Come as living stones and let yourselves be used in building the spiritual temple.'

1Peter 2-5

Don't give me much
I'll only want more

Don't come too close
just stay like before

Public and stoic
and terribly British

Don't look away
just give me a smile

I know all the while in your gaze
is a maze of emotion

Build up your wall
but use me for the stones

Stay buttoned and tight but
let me be the bones

to lengthen
and strengthen
your coping.

May 27th

Zechariah to be known as Zac, the announcement of a new arrival in school!

Old biblical names are quite fashionable again now, especially for boys. Joshua, Benjamin, Daniel, Zac, Jacob, Saul, Eli. Joel.

What a rich heritage these little guys have to call on if they get interested enough to find out a bit more about their namesakes.

Joshua – Leader of the Israelites from the Hebrew 'Yehoshu'a' which means Yahweh is salvation.

Benjamin – Founder of one of the twelve tribes whose name means favoured son of the right hand.

Daniel – Hebrew prophet whose name means God is my judge

Zac – from Zechariah, father of John the Baptist, name also means salvation.

Jacob – father of Israel whose name means supplanter.

Saul – means asked for or prayed for.

Eli - High priest of Israel and teacher of Samuel whose name means ascension.

Joel – Old Testament prophet, Hebrew name Yo'el meaning Yahweh or salvation.

Father may the significance of their names empower these children as they grow and become adults in an ever changing and bewildering world.

May 28th

Father when the earthquake wrenched open the prison doors on Paul and Silas, they didn't make a bid for freedom. Acts 16 26-30

How did Paul and Silas, who had been praying and singing praises to God, know that they were to remain in their ruined cell?

Why did they not interpret the unlocking of their door as divine intervention for their freedom?

Clearly as we read on we see that they were instrumental in bringing the gospel message to the jailer and his family and doing far more good than if they had just escaped into the night.

Teach me to wait, to discern your purposes for me rather than rush headlong into the first idea which comes into my head after I have prayed.

May 29th

'This is the day the Lord has made.'

In the power of Christ and open to receive, through the Holy Spirit, communion with our Lord God, I sit in quiet expectation.

Expectant and still; in the knowledge that He is here with me.

Graciously grant me the time today to be with you, alone.

May 30th

I kissed an elderly friend goodbye recently and was struck by the beautiful, peach like, quality of her face. With ninety decades under her belt and probably not much in the way of a beauty regime, she had the skin of a child. Her wonderfully twinkling eyes and ready smile; her ever gracious acceptance of all that life has brought her, has given her a radiance which no artist could capture. She is an inspiration to everyone who meets her.

Her years have been punctuated with hard work, a large family; and all the ups and downs, the attendant tears and laughter which have come with it. She has known a lot of making do and mending, not much luxury or indulgence and yet has been content; content in all things because of her unshakable faith.

Her practice has been to recite the 23 psalm each day.

My friend is as open and honest and trusting as a child.

She has the faith of a child, pure and unquestioning.

Yet she is not gullible, she is wise,

She is not simple she is prudent, practical and discreet.

I cannot help but think that it is she who holds the secret of eternal youth, the key to the longevity we as a society seem to seek.

The Lord is my shepherd; therefore what could I possibly lack?

May 31st

I feel I want to think more on the 23rd Psalm today, it is so very wonderful.

The Lord is my shepherd; I lack for nothing.

He makes me lie down in green pastures; he leads me to water where I may rest;

He revives my spirit; for his name's sake he guides me in the right paths.

Even if were to walk through a valley of deepest darkness

I should fear no harm, for you are with me;

Your shepherd's staff and crook afford me comfort.

You spread a table for me in the presence of my enemies;

you have anointed my head with oil and my cup brims over.

Goodness and love unfailing will follow me all the days of my life

And I will dwell in the house of the Lord throughout the years to come.

Revised English Bible

Amen

June 1st

Summer is here and who can beat an English summer?

The municipal parks are glorious and freely open for everyone to enjoy.

Gardens are ablaze with every shade and hue jostling to be noticed.

Balconies on flats show off collections of pots and containers, their brightly coloured contents climbing up and over the railings, threatening to spill out to freedom.

The trees are a testament to their own self importance, who can argue with something which reminds a mere human of their mortality?

Great God I stand in awesome appreciation of all that which is good and which restores my soul and enriches my life.

Great God I am happily reminded of the extent of your providence.

Great God I stand in admiration before you and rejoice.

June 2nd

Lord am I really ready to do your will?

How much do I really mean it when I say 'here I am Lord, send me'?

You know the mental caveats I put on my spoken words, you know just how much I hold back.

I am embarrassed to acknowledge my meanness of spirit whilst at the same time being only too ready to accept the grateful words of those with whom I do come into contact for you.

Lord I know that you will test us in our faith,

but only so that we may grown to know you better,

trust you more surely and live for you more generously.

Clear my heart of its excuses and help me to say unreservedly

'here I am Lord, send me'.

June 3rd

'The wisdom of the ancients', how often we hear that phrase applied to one set of philosophies or another.

I wonder though, did they know they were being wise at the time or has the appreciation of the precision of their observations only come about over centuries of analysis and experience?

Was in fact the hypothesis which they proposed actually derided in their own time?

Was the theory on which they practiced their empiricism accepted in their own time?

Are there people here and now, in this new millennium, whose knowledge and opinion we should be revering more?

Heavenly Father there is more media coverage of more informed and uninformed opinion than there has ever been at any other time in history. Help me to disseminate fact from fiction, truth from lie, hyperbole from plain, understated yet well informed knowledge.

June 4th

In praying yesterday for my own need to understand and trust the right opinions, I thought about the bigger picture of world leaders and peace brokers. Father they have to rely on the integrity of professional research teams to make informed decisions which affect us all.

Lord, in whose keeping we trust and in whose great benevolence we believe, please grant to those in positions of power, at national and international level, clarity, honesty and unambiguous courage, to work for a better world for us all.

June 5th

Have I got news for you, could I Mastermind Tomorrow's World for you by asking Who Wants to be a Millionaire? I don't mean Deal or no Deal. Would you like A House in the Sun or some Relocation? How about a night with Friends or a few beers at Cheers!

Are you a Casualty of too many Points of View? Do you feel like The Weakest Link in this Sea of Souls, this Quest for, search for Celebrity status?

Surprise Surprise!

Take it or leave it.

Here's a new programme to demonstrate how more money, more fame, a bigger house, a better house, a new house somewhere else, will not influence but might well hinder God's plan for your life.

But that wouldn't make very good viewing would it?

June 6th

It's a cruel fool
who spurns the love of God.
A mean spirit
with no time to spare,
for salvation hanging there
on a cross in front of him.

It's a cruel fool
who ignores with confidence
the sanctifying spirit,
who walks away
doesn't hear Him say
'Come to me'.

It's a humble soul
who takes the love of God.
An open spirit
with time to spare
to clasp salvation hanging there
on a cross in front of him.

It's a humble soul
who accepts with expectation
the dove, the Holy Spirit.
Who with trusting faith, not seeing
finds a new eternal way of being
and says 'I come'.

June 7th

I proclaim and give thanks for my faith and the liberation that worshiping Jesus Christ as God and Saviour brings to me.

I would not like it if my prayer times were prescribed as in Islam and yet I envy the Islamic dedication.

I envy the complete obedience to prayer.

I admire the rule about coming 'clean' before God and the ritual washing, even inside the mouth, that what comes out of it might be wholesome and pleasing to Allah.

I appreciate the opening phrase in praise and thanksgiving to God, set words of supplication and adoration, all uttered in faith that, through devoutness, unspoken issues and personal problems will be attended to.

Father God, help us appreciate and respect those of other faiths whose ways, although different from ours, are no less sincere and holy, and from which we might learn.

June 8th

Tadpole to frog, chrysalis to butterfly, acorn to oak tree, all changes which defy probability yet they happen as if without effort.

Faith the size of a mustard seed, that's all we need,

we are told in Matthew 17:19-20 and Luke 17:5-6.

How big is a mustard seed?   ....   Well, there are 12 of them!

Does not that defy probability? Does that not test our comprehension?

Does not that demonstrate the almighty power of God, who can hear and work on prayers from a faith so small?

June 9th

Lord I was inspired today to speak up for those of us who had faithfully prayed for someone.

On being given the all clear from her illness and its attendant worries a colleague said what a 'lucky' person she was, how she had come through the last few months she just didn't know!!

My response was a bit sharp and less Christ like than it should have been as I pointed out, albeit with a smile, that the power of prayer might have had something to do with it.

Said as it was I think it sounded mean and not prayerful at all.

If I am going to speak out for you grant me patient understanding and a more gracious tone.

June 10th

I have been recommended a book which advertises its contents as:-

> 'Mentoring policies and procedures, skills of delegation, planning strategies and relationship structuring'

I am not immediately drawn to it I have to say, despite it being much vaunted in the work place as a 'modern day bible for successful corporate management'.

The Holy Bible exhorts mentoring; the Old Testament has Jethro suggesting a change in management techniques to Moses in the book of Exodus. Boaz shows tremendous leadership and 'relationship management' in the book of Ruth when he fulfils the obligations of his tribe and family. Jesus, throughout the whole of the New Testament teaches and leads from the front. Dealing with people with firmness, compassion, kindliness, even extreme anger when he turned over the money changers' tables in the Temple. His 'delegation techniques' as he encourages and develops the potential in his disciples is perfect.

There is nothing new. The thirst for answers to the majority of today's situations can be met in The Bible. All mentoring polices and procedures, skills of delegation, planning strategies and relationship structuring advice with examples. All the key life skills advice anyone could ever need, written and recorded on papyrus and vellum a very long time ago.

June 11th

Father, loving Lord, please lead me through the mountain of printed material written by people who, in all good faith, are sharing their experiences. Help me to recognise and accept advice and the benefit of expertise where I need it and where it will benefit me; but Father, help me to stand firm against that which will undermine or take me from your way of doing things.

June 12th

Risen, ascended Lord,

grant me the insight to fully **know** and understand the meaning in that address.

Risen, ascended Lord,

grant me the insight to fully know and **understand** the meaning in that address.

Risen, ascended Lord,

I rejoice in your triumph.

June 13th

New beginnings all around
New beginnings now abound
New beginning Lord I see
New beginnings here for me.

    New beginnings all the time
    New beginnings joy divine
    New beginnings Lord I see
    New beginnings here for me.

        If only I'd look properly.

June 14th

Lord confirm and strengthen me in the work you have set before me.

Help me to seek out those you have identified for me to be with.

Help me to be more active in my efforts to share the good news of Jesus.

Help me to show, by my life, what having a living faith can mean.

Lord as hearts break behind smiles, as loneliness cripples behind stiff upper lips,

> *help me to know and go where you send me.*

Lord as rejection is hidden behind brave words and abuse behind excuses,

> *help me to hear your prompting and go where you need me.*

Lord confirm and strengthen me.

Give me the guidance and power of the Holy Spirit to set out on my ministry for you today.

June 15th

The love of the Lord Jesus Christ is the gift which we are given on our acceptance of His rule in our lives and it is this love which we must give ourselves if we are to be whole and called Children of the Living Lord.

We must treat ourselves with all the passion we put into loving Him for we are His.

We must seek out the good in ourselves and celebrate Him in us.

We must whisper sweet words of encouragement, gentle words of sustenance as He would.

We must honour and give reverence to that love in us as we do to Him.

We are children of the Living Lord we must radiate the love which is in the Lord our Saviour.

We are carriers of the most precious gift, love.

June 16th

These early summer days are lulling me into a sense of peace and healing, a feeling that law, order and harmony might be possible for everyone, everywhere.

How deceptive my perceptions are when all is lovely in my own moment of time.

I do appreciate this feeling of contentment though.

I acknowledge that all is not well for many millions of people.

Mostly though, I just want this lovely little oasis in my own little corner of the world, to exist for a while longer.

There are weeds, there is a broken fence, there are lots of jobs to be getting on with, yet I sit.

I sit and 'be still' for the presence of the Lord is here in this place with me and I can hardly breathe for fear of disturbing the moment.

The full pollen sacs on the legs of the bees, the smell of the mock orange, the prism through the dew drop deep inside the delphinium cup, the tenuous beauty of a day lily; oh Lord I could cry at the breathtaking magic.

Help me to take all these manifestations of your glory into my heart and into my memory bank to be drawn on when things get me down.

June 17th

I have to go to a meeting today Lord which I am not looking forward to.

I have to hear what people have to say on a subject about which I feel very strongly.

I have to try to compare and contrast their many views and then in one or two sentences produce a succinct consensus.

Father grant me the wisdom of Solomon as I try to wrest, from all the fevered postulation, a way forward.

Help me to be fair and impartial, to decipher and decide the best path to take and Father above all help me to promote a feeling of acceptance and importance to all the points of view.

Help me to encourage an atmosphere of trust and respect in remembrance that what we all seek is your will and the common good.

Lord prepare me for the fray, and as I put on the armour of the Lord I know that you will be very near and ever with me.

June 18th

Next week we will go to a funeral, the dear wife of a university friend. It has affected all my family deeply, not only because a friend is no longer with us but it has reminded everyone that we won't always be around for each other.

For those of us with faith we have the blessed assurance of a home in heaven and our Father God waiting but for those with no such faith we must pray especially.

What to pray for though?

The Lord will always meet them at their point of need even if they don't recognise it. He can and does smooth troubled waters and grieving hearts.

For me personally it is a bitter sweet feeling and I must confess that although safe in my faith and ultimate celestial destination, I am not ready to leave my earthly life just yet. I have much I still want to do and many people whose presence in my life I love and want to continue to enjoy for years to come, God willing.

Thankfully, God wasn't willing to prolong our friend's earthly life, she was so sick and we can rejoice at her liberation from pain. We can also celebrate her treasured life on earth and her arrival in heaven.

June 19th

Each new second is a chance to begin again

Each new minute is an opportunity to begin again

Each new hour is an occasion to begin again

Each new day is a miracle.

Each miracle deserves to be acknowledged

Each miracle warrants recognition

Recognition means credit

Recognition means gratitude

Recognition means appreciation.

Appreciation shows a conscious

awareness of each new beginning.

June 20th

In 1 Corinthians, Chapter 12 Paul speaks of the body not being of one part but of many and that no one part of the body is less valuable than the other. In unison, when all parts of the body are working together, doing God's work, then we are able to realize His vision.

Lord, help me to realise the value of everyone I meet.

May I recognise in them a living part of the body of Christ.

May I honour and respect them as a part of that body, holy and cherished by you.

May I see in them the beautiful, special, unique character that is your creation.

June 21st

Long days and short nights, Oh the joy of extra daylight.

As we approach the longest day, the passage of time seems amplified.

It seems as though spring has barely finished and summer really still in its infancy and yet we are on the inexorable march towards autumn.

Isn't the way of things? Isn't that life?

It was only a couple of years ago that the children were home for the holidays, or was it only a couple of years ago that they went to university. No, I remember, it was just a couple of years ago that we were arranging weddings. Hey even before all that, I was young and in love, that only seems like a couple of years ago too in some ways.

Now there are 2 little grandsons to mark the march of years, never mind seasons.

Oh dear Father God may I treasure every season of the year and of my life. As I make a more Christ centred effort day by day and appreciate the changes, I know that I am in your loving plan whatever the seasonal fluctuations.

June 27th

Does that mother, eyes swollen from crying
as her husband carries that little rag wrapped corpse
to it's grave, know that here
on the other side of the world, a continent away
another mother saw her war torn, war ravaged,
war weary, heart broken face on the television
and cried with her?
Does that mother, sitting in the dry sterile
dust bowl she once called land offering a shrivelled
empty breast to a goggle eyed baby
whose distended belly belies the
 hunger and starvation inside,
know that another mother on the other side of the world
 is wreathed in guilt as she scrapes
her children's left-overs into the bin
tears streaming, conscience screaming?

Does that mother, sacrificing her children
on the alter of frustrated material, maternal ambition
ever wonder if in manipulating ego
she is hammering another nail in the coffin
of those whose expectation
is just to live?

What if they were to know?
could begin to know,
those mothers on the other

side of the world;
would they cry for their sophisticated sisters' turmoil?
Or would they cry with relief at the
simplicity of their own desires?

Lord will the prayers, donations and efforts of so many generous people around the world ever really affect the horrors of those in such dire need?

June 28th

I was going to go shopping today but after the trials of my thoughts yesterday I will make do. I have a well stocked freezer and a store cupboard so I know I have more than enough, not just for today but for several days.

Thank you Father for making me stop and think, thank you for making me take time look more deeply about how I do things.

Lord I do pray that the corruption, in countries we so earnestly seek to support, will soon be a thing of the past and that we will see a healthy renewal of dignity and life amongst all peoples.

June 29th

To have faith is to be sure of the things we hope for; to be certain of the things we cannot see.   Heb 11:1

I pray today for all those for whom this verse has little relevance.

For those in such pain that they know there is no God.

For those in deepest depression whose world is black, desperate and Godless.

For those who are so lonely that the endless time spent in solitude feels like a terminal sentence.

Lord Jesus who reached out to sick and lame, to tormented and persecuted; comfort and strengthen those who feel alone. Be with those who are so isolated in their circumstances that they are trapped in their own living hell.

May they, through some small thing that happens today, be taken out of themselves for a brief spell to see the light, to smell fresh air to have a respite from their agony.

Lord in you all things are possible.   Amen.

June 30th

I do love the garden Lord, weeding or sitting, planning or planting and there have been so many notable quotes from those who acknowledge your hand in their efforts.

I think that if ever a mortal heard the voice of God it would be in a garden at the cool of the day.
FFMoore – A Garden of Peace

Plants give us oxygen for the lungs and soul.
Linda Solego

Count your garden by the flowers, never by the leaves that fall.
Count your days by the golden hours, don't remember clouds at all.
Count your life by smiles, not tears, and with joy on every birthday.
Count your age by friends, not years.
Anon

The kiss of the sun for pardon,
The song of the birds for mirth,--
One is nearer God's heart in a garden
Than anywhere else on earth.
Dorothy Francis Gurney

My green thumb came only as result of the mistakes I made whilst learning to see things from the plant's point of view.
Fred Ale

July 1st

Saint Gall Day -also known as Gal; still a pretty awful name for such an amazing man, from Gallic I assume.

St Gall was of Gallic nobility and a relative of Saint Vettius Apagatus, the Uncle and teacher of St Gregory of Tours. He refused an arranged marriage to the daughter of an imperial senator, and withdrew to the monastery at Cournon near Auvergne. He was known as a miracle worker, and as a man so meek and humble that those who sought to attack him were often converted by his gentleness.

We know so little about this man Lord yet he was clearly very special and what a wonderful testament to his life! Even just to be remembered almost two millennia later for being 'so meek and humble that those who sought to attack him were often converted by his gentleness'.

What might an epitaph say about me? Would it have anyone stop in their tracks in two thousand years time?

July 2nd

May the God of peace provide you with every good thing you need in order to do His will.   Heb.13:21

Dear Father of all, your teaching through the Bible is such a constant in my life. How clearly I am brought to account in this verse and how easily I might slip passed the denouement. 'in order to do **His** will'.

That God would provide us with every good thing is fine, thank you God, but read on, only that which is needed in order to do His will. If we realise that in doing His will we are doing what our Lord commanded of us then it is good and what we do in His name is good and so God will honour that effort.

Lord, life in you is rich indeed and each day walking with you a joy. Help me to be ever available to do your will, as you lead me.

July 3rd

Father, there are so many fund raising events going on around the country at this time, school end of term concerts, summer fetes in villages, sponsored walks and challenges. Please bless all those who give their time so generously to accomplish these meetings. None of them happens without a great deal of behind the scenes work of committees and bodies of willing folk. Help us to appreciate the unsung heroes without whom the charities would be very much worse off.

In a world where it is easy to become cynical and dispirited at the pace of change help us to keep faith and keep supporting.

Thank you for the commitment shown by loyal, steadfast supporters who bring about great benefit to us all by their tireless work.

July 4th

Holy Spirit, ignite in me your holy fire
that I might work to lovingly inspire
others to know you.

Holy Spirit, ignite in me your holy fire
that I might help others to acquire
a thirst for you.

Holy Spirit, ignite in me your holy fire
that I might, with the angel choir
open ears to you.

July 5th

Loving Lord, thank you for showing me that it isn't you coming as a magician with a wand which will achieve all the things I ask for but that my entreaties for a better, kinder heart, a purer way of thinking, a more Christ like way of dealing with people, will be brought about by you showing me how.

It is you who will guide and help me to amend my ways; your spirit will lead me to affect the changes I pray for.

Sorry I'm so stubborn.

July 6th

Oh Father I am angry today and I can barely come before you, certainly not with an open and contrite heart.

The news this morning is of another young soldier killed. Another family plunged into deep, mourning.

I know it is by the evil deeds of sinful man that these atrocities are perpetrated; I know that you are weeping with the families, supporting them in their grief but WHY?

Why did it have to happen? Why does it keep on happening?

What good purpose does all this unrest serve apart from bringing the next generation up to think that it is the normal way of going about things?

What must we do Lord? Oh for God's sake what must we do?

What can I do? Yes I know I pray; but just now it really doesn't seem like peace is at the top of anyone else's agenda.

Please, from the depths of my frustration and abject helplessness, may we see some constructive and lasting paths to peace and reconciliation in the war torn areas of this beautiful world.

July 7th

Forgive my outburst yesterday Lord I pray.

Like a petulant child I flung off into the rest of my day completely feeding on my anger and indignation, I certainly didn't feel connected to you at all. And why? Because instead of coming to you in quiet, gentle confusion I railed and cried and spent the rest of the day in self inflicted misery.

Your arms were what I wanted, the comfort, the strength, the security, which faith in you allows me access to.

Today I feel like a shoe the dog once found washed up on the beach. It was perfectly functional but a bit battered. It needed a bit of TLC, taking home drying off and then polishing to restore it to its leather best. Had she found the other one there would have been serviceable footwear for someone.

Father dry my tears and restore me to my spiritual best today.

Accept my prayer and may I feel the peace for your forgiveness.

I ask this in Jesus name.   Amen.

July 8th

I love preparing the house and garden for people's arrival. Whether it is guests for a quiet day, friends or family, I just relish getting ready. I am always prepared for an unexpected visitor but when the arrangements have been made ahead of time I can make an extra special effort. I do the things that I appreciate when I go visiting: flowers or a scented candle burning in my room, a thoughtfully chosen book by the bed, a new bar of soap to luxuriate with in a relaxing bath.

Then of course there is the food to be planned, we never feel we can just serve up what we would have for a mid-week supper do we? So the planning of menus and baking of goodies, only permitted on high days and holidays, like cake and pastries.

What would I do if I knew Jesus was coming to stay?

What would I do if I opened the door and he was standing there, looking for a bed for the night?

Mary or Martha?

Would I fly round trying to get everything in order or would I just sit at his feet in wonderment and adoration.

I know he is here all the time in our home but do I always do my best by him?

I don't think he would want a fuss, I think he would just want me to be myself, the self he made, without pretension or affectation.

I hope we could have cake though!

July 9th

'Thoughts alight as the humour moves them' Robert Louis Stevenson on Railway travel.

What a luxury to lie in the shade of a large tree and day dream. Let thoughts meander in and out of reach, from the practical to the absurd, from the fantastical to the mundane.

I wonder if RLS meant as the 'sense of humour' moved them. Sometimes we see the ridiculous in very ordinary things; sometimes we don't see the funny side of a joke or situation at all. Or did he mean humours as in bodily fluid? Medieval science and medicine placed great store by the balance of blood, yellow bile, black bile and lymph.

We all need time to think, to formulate ideas to 'chew the fat' with ourselves. Thinking is important and I worry that we don't have enough time for it in today's world. I especially worry that our children are not given enough thinking time. I wonder if this may ultimately impinge, on their ability to critically analyse the pros and cons of a circumstance before making a decision.

So it was a luxury to lie in the warm shade and cogitate, all in the name of my research and in order to balance my humours of course!

July 10th

Summer days seem made for reading, I certainly try to take every opportunity to be outside with my work or a book and there seems to be a fresh perspective, a new diligence to my efforts when I am in contact with grass and trees. My senses seem sharper and my eyes clearer. Perhaps that is why Brother Ramon's words about 'adoration' made such an impression on me.

He was writing about making adoration a part of our meditative time with God and the fruits of that effort being that:

> 'We shall be struck down with the wonder and majesty of God; we shall be melted by his love and transfigured by his glory'.
>
> Deeper into God : Bro Ramon

Struck down, melted, transfigured! This is very physical, passionate writing.

I think I need to give more time to the adoration part of my worship.

July 11th

Father I write with such ease about appreciating your word and world from my garden; about being healed by the presence of grass and trees; about being able to pray whilst walking the dog by the river or across the fields. I know though, that so very many of my fellow Christian brothers and sisters worship you from their high rise apartments, their streets of houses, their balconies and their amazing communities within communities; outside means pavements and people and traffic and noise.

I enjoy that dynamic, I really enjoy going up to the city and being a part of it and I celebrate life in the myriad faces I see. I appreciate the immediacy of '24/7' shops and cinema and theatre and so many churches to choose from! I go green with envy at the availability of public transport and the choice of restaurants, 'every nationality here represented' as they say in the United Nation's toast.

I pray that as a race we can learn to appreciate our differences. I pray that we can respect and hold in due reverence those ideals and opinions which are important to our neighbours.

July 12th

Don't let the
shine of your
moondust only
settle on others.

Don't let the
warmth of your
sun only give
life to others.

Don't let the
vessel of your
precious self become
drained by others.

When moonshine falls
on you
harvest it
for you.

When radiance warms
you
store it
for you.

And when you can
be filled
with the
Spirit of God.

July 13th

I dedicate all that I do today to you Lord, may I radiate your love.

Help me to have you in the forefront of everything, every conversation and act.

May all that I do and say be acceptable to you.

Help me to remember this pledge before I leave the safety of my home.

Help me to remember this prayer as I encounter the traffic on the main road into Cambridge.

Help me to remember this hope as I struggle through the crowds of tourists in the market place.

Help me to remember this and try to live it out.

I know before too long that I will fail.

The traffic is always bad and there is always one bright spark who thinks they know the road better than the rest of us. I will have grimaced and gurned before I have restrained myself.

There are always thousands of tourists around the city at this time of year and we need the revenue that they bring with them but I won't remember this as I try to hurtle through their leisurely perambulations. I will puff and tut with self inflated indignation as I go by.

I dedicate everything I do today to you Lord, may I radiate your love with a smile. May all that I do be acceptable to you and may I greet every situation with the expectancy that something good will ensue.

July 14th

The liberation of Jerusalem in the First Crusade 1095.

Jerusalem's history is one of deep heartache and bloodshed for everyone of whatever doctrinal persuasion. It is the beating heart on which the world gazes for its religious focus; the symbol of tortured faith and mutilated hope. Yet, to see its physical presence, the walls, the domes, the crosses, the stars of David is to feel optimism. One feels that goodness could yet forge a path through the dogmatism of division.

I feel that the righting of peace to Jerusalem will be a seminal moment in bringing peace to the world and I pray for it, with all my soul.

July 15th

You who are too big for me to know

You who are too great for me to comprehend

You who are too omnipotent for me to understand

You who are too supreme for me to truly appreciate

You who are too powerful for me to grasp

You have given me Jesus and made the impossible possible.

Through him I can know you

Through him I can begin to comprehend

Through him I can start to understand

Through him I can learn to appreciate

Through him I can truly grasp

      the love God has for me.

July 16th

It has been a long time since Easter. A very long time since the first Easter and I want to remind myself today of the glorious liberation I feel every Easter Day when we shout with one voice,

> 'Hosanna, He is Risen, Hallelujah'

It is important to celebrate and remember that every day.

It is our Risen Lord who meets us at our place of prayer.

It is our Risen Lord to whom we address our supplications and praise.

It is the Easter person inside each one of us who profess the Christian faith.

It is the Easter message which propels us with joy and burning desire to hear the world cry,

> 'Hosanna, He is Risen, Hallelujah'.

Let's not confine church festivals to a calendar but live them every day.

July 17th

Do atheists pray I wonder?

When those who profess no faith suddenly cry 'My God' as an exclamation, does God accept that as a salutation.

In the same vein, 'Good Lord' or 'Heavens Above' are used with no real thought other than as an expletive, but what does God make of it? Are these still prayers?

More importantly, does the person uttering these words have a deep seated desire for there to be a God listening?

As I have made a more conscious effort to notice so I am amazed at the number of times people with no faith refer to a supreme being in their discourse. Committed members of a faith do not do it out of respect and a conviction that it is blasphemy.

There is a modern trend in unpleasant profanity taking the name of Jesus Christ in vain and I find this upsetting. Why though should I find it any worse than the 'Oh my God' expression?

Lord as people use your name in their exclamations and expletives may they be minded to think on what they have just done and give you a moment's thought.

July 18th

Am I guilty of giving more or less reverence to the individual parts of the Trinity?

After thinking about my feelings yesterday I wondered why I would find a sacrilegious outburst against Jesus and Jesus Christ more offensive that against God. How would I react if suddenly the modern parlance was to invoke the Holy Spirit as an expletive?

I would be appalled and want to make my feelings evident.

Dear Lord forgive me for my unbelief, forgive me I pray for my mean dilution of the power of God the Father, Three in One. Forgive me for my lack of understanding about a concept which is known through faith and faith alone.

Teach me Lord, more of the mysteries of faith and of your power, through God the Father God the Son and God the Holy Spirit.   Amen.

July 19th

What an answer to prayer! I politely asked a young Muslim student I know not to use the name of God as an exclamation. She looked a bit non-plussed to start with. I asked if she would take the name of Allah in vain and of course she strenuously objected, so I said how it hurt me to hear God's name being used as an expletive. She was very contrite and said she had never thought of it in that way before but would try to think twice in future about blaspheming in any holy person's name.

I pray that I will always have the right words and courage to gently challenge when I find myself in that situation again but I guess I won't always have such a sympathetic ear!

July 20th

'The best way to cheer yourself up is to cheer someone else up'   Mark Twain

That works in reverse too!

This morning I went out with a joyous summer heart then I met someone I know well who is crumbling with real problems and I have come home deeply troubled.

Father I bring my friend's burdens to the foot of your cross.

I pray for him in his time of great distress and ask that you will be able to comfort him in a way which brings some relief. I pray that although concerned, the things I learned will not drag me down to the point where I am no good.

Lord as we bring to your all embracing arms those we love, give us the faith to let go and leave them in your tender care.

July 21st

Eternity waits for me in heaven. I don't take it for granted but I work towards it and pray that, as I walk with The Lord and sanctified by his grace, I will become worthy of my place when the time comes. It seems odd to some people that as Christians we appear to do all that we do here on earth in order to secure our life in the hereafter; not that I am thinking about that day by day.

I know as a non believer one is just as conscientious about looking after ones fellow man, doing good, respecting the planet but the thought that, the end is the end, is of course incomprehensible to those with faith.

There has been much written, not always sympathetically, about the security blanket of faith being for those who don't want to grow up and face reality.

I would turn the argument around and suggest that proclaiming not to have any faith is a naive option which involves only man made structure and stricture and absolves one from any form of responsibility to anything other than human frailty, therefore far from perfect.

We have to live our lives on this earth but I thank the Lord that ultimately I shall be in a place which is flawless, and *I* will be too.

July 22nd

I have had a bit of heaven on earth today and it seems extra special after my thoughts on eternity yesterday. I adore lemon curd; I am the only one in my family who does and I went to a coffee morning where I spied a beautiful lemon sponge cake with lemon curd filling. There was a wonderful selection of home baking to buy, lots of things the rest of my family would enjoy, but I bought the lemon cake. I was like a child bursting with expectation as I cycled home with the sponge in my bicycle basket, salivating at the thought of a cup of strong black coffee and a piece of the sweet cake.

 I rushed in and began to make my coffee, I unpeeled the cellophane and set the cake on a plate and just looked at it. What a lot of ingredients and love had brought it into being.

Someone had carefully weighed ingredients and chosen eggs, beaten and blended, buttered and baked it to perfection; then, just for me, had filled it with a gloriously rich lemon curd.

I wish I could say I felt guilty as I sat down to my indulgence but I truly didn't. I gave thanks and then surrendered myself into a little bit of heaven right there at my kitchen table.

July 23rd

Father I pray for our church leaders. I feel confused and saddened at the turmoil within your church. I feel insecure and unstable at the division within the body of Christ here on earth. The church seems to take so much care to appeal to and reach everyone that you, the Lord God of all and your message of redemption, seem to be being sidelined, away from any meaningful existence.

Give me discernment to follow debate and understand diverse viewpoints but ultimately give me the will to trust those whom you have chosen to work for you.

Give me the faith to trust that, empowered by the Holy Spirit; they will bring about your kingdom here on earth.

Holy Holy Holy Lord.   Amen.

July 24th

Envelope me in your presence
and transport me to the place
where I feel the heat
from the heart of God.
Consume me in the folds
of your atmosphere
where only our oneness
is tangible.
Smother me in a jubilant rapture
and blind me with the
heavenly light of the
Holy Spirit.
Fill me with an all consuming passion
which will irradiate
and transfigure me into
a spiritual being.

July 25th

I do get a great deal of joy from watching the birds in my garden.

I probably spend far too much time and money on them, the array of different foods for different birds that I have at the ready. As a child we only ever put out a few crumbs or a bit of bacon rind and very occasionally half a coconut if the fair had been to town. The table cloth was always taken to the door to be given a good shake so there might have been a few pickings there. Now there are seeds and grains for every breed and time of year.

Have we made the birds lazy? Have we changed the ecological balance of avian life in our quest to tempt a wider and more diverse selection of birds into our gardens or onto our balconies?

I think that birds are more opportunistic than we take them for and more savvy about their own wellbeing.

So, thank you Lord for the pleasure we get from the birds who share our space, through them we learn so much about the diversity and joy in your creation.

July 26th

'Then he opened their minds so that they could understand the scriptures'
Luke 24:45

Jesus, just as you opened the minds of your disciples in Jerusalem, please give me the understanding and perception to read and truly digest your word. I pray that the Holy Spirit will peel back the scales from my mind, that I might grasp your message as I study my Bible day by day. Empower me with the significance of what I learn and direct me in the use of that knowledge to your praise and glory.

July 27th

Thank you for hens, my hens in particular. I found one of the ladies trying out for the gymnastics team on the fence this morning. Head and neck held high, superior look on her face; she wobbled three feet above the other girls as much as to say 'the gold medal is mine'. The chain link was bowing under her weight as she tottered along it, it is a real pity she is an egg layer and not destined for the dinner table. When I asked her what she was doing she looked at me with her head on one side as much as to say, 'now who's the pea brain'. The thing is, I know that my ladies are philosophers. I know that in their clucking they are actually evaluating many of the issues of the world which perplex the rest of us and they probably get some answers too. Although it may seem strange I do feel a real sense of rightness when I'm with them. Their perspective is one of immediacy, is there some food? Can they have a bit of fuss and a scratch behind the ears?…not unlike the dog!

How we need these levellers in our lives to restore a rhythm and measure to the pattern of our days.

So Lord, thank you for my hens and the joy and the eggs which they bring.

July 28th

Almost the end of another month.

Father, tempus fugit with all that we seem to feel is important, with all that we seem to think makes us indispensable, invaluable and insufferably smug.

How much better it seems if we are rushed off our feet, how much more worthwhile our lives appear if they are full from morning to night; if we have to factor into our diaries a quick word with a colleague or a cup of coffee with a friend.

How appreciated and self satisfied is our exhaustion when we can be truly martyred on the altar of our schedules?

I hear you shouting STOP.

STOP being so resoundingly insecure that you feel the need to have to be seen being busy.

So, Father God, help me to seek your presence this coming week end through the enjoyment of my garden, my books and the company of my loved ones take time to appreciate the small private things about which no one else will know or judge me for.

I will read the papers and share the space you have given me with a relaxed heart knowing that you ordained a day of rest for us all.

July 29th

After yesterdays insight into my personal scheduling I changed my plans for today and STOPPED. As I tried to do the crossword with my breakfast I realised that I had doodled a whole margin of day dreams. The doodles made me think of art, not those specifically, and I remembered my paint box.

Suffice it to say that the next 4 hours passed in glorious absorption as I colour washed flowers and thoughts onto the paper.

There is nothing to exhibit.

There is nothing which would have any meaning or relevance to anyone else.

However, the cathartic effect of that time was as good as a retreat to my soul.

I became rested and peacefully empty of all the niggles which were beginning to seem insurmountable.

I imagine potters forming lumps of clay around their reflections get the same inspiration and I know that poetry, when it flows, brings creation through contemplation.

I will try and STOP again soon.

July 30th

'In calm detachment lies your safety, your strength in quiet trust.' Is.30:15

Today's bible study verse seems ridiculously apposite after the last couple of day's thoughts because I did hand myself into his safe keeping for those few hours of detachment.

We can rest in His peace, for which we are truly grateful, and be confident that in Him we will be brought through to share the glory of His presence.

July 31st

We have just been to a murder mystery dinner and had such fun. We were all given our persona for the evening ahead of time so that we could get into role and come well briefed. We were told what to wear and what our past history had been. We were even told about various moments and situations in our private lives which might compromise the truth of other peoples witness statements. All we had to do then, apart from interact with the other guests was to enjoy a lovely meal and answer the questions as put to us by the 'investigating officer' in charge of the case. We all had a very pleasurable and cheerful evening with the murderer being identified through a process of elimination of the rest of us.

One of the guests asked the hypothetical question:

'Wouldn't life be easy if we were given the brief before hand?'

And so I wondered if, instead of meeting each new situation and having to make choices, we could walk a prescribed route. Wouldn't life be easier if instead of having free will we were fed the lines to meet each individual circumstance so that we didn't need to worry about the right and wrong of anything?'

There was much light hearted banter but actually the more I thought about it afterwards the more I think we do have a blue print for meeting all life's situations.

Lord I will always have choices to make but I know I am never alone and that I can bring every situation, however difficult, to you before I make a decision.

August 1st

Lord I sit in the quiet of this place and come to you.

Lord I sit in the quiet of this place and wait on you.

Lord I sit in the quiet of this place and know that

the power of the Holy Spirit will fill me to overflowing

with your love.

August 2nd

Enlightenment.

The Enlightenment was an eighteenth century movement in Europe which advocated 'Reason' as the primary basis of authority. Reason means that all statements should have an empirical or sense observed foundation.

In Buddhism it is the state attained when reincarnation is finished and desire and suffering are transcended.

Lord I use the word to seek to learn about you and how I might become more like the person you want me to be. There are things which I will never be able to prove empirically because they are of the heart and the soul but they are very real and reasonable to me. So Lord, enlighten me, explain to me, illuminate me, show me more of the grace of Jesus I pray.

August 3rd

Father in heaven I ask that you will anoint me with the oil of your gracious forgiveness.

I recognise the times that I have let you down knowingly with a harsh word or uncharitable thought.

I know that there are times when I let you down unknowingly, thoughtlessly and with arrogant abandon.

Forgive me I pray and set a right heart in me.   Amen

August 4th

As the wedding bells ring out in the village I pray for couples everywhere being married in this glorious summer sunshine. I extend the famous prayer of in the Sarum Missal of 1497.

'God be in their heads and in their understanding'

Develop patience, kindness and grace in their relationship, as they grow together over the coming years.

'God be in their eyes and in their looking'

Enable them to see and appreciate each other's needs and to meet them with loving dedication and tenderness. Help them to see the beauty in simple pleasures and quiet times as well as in the splendid excitement of a day like today.

'God be in their mouths and in their speaking'

that respect and consideration will moderate harsh or hurtful words which demoralise and damage. Guide them in the ways of encouragement and kindness which will build and nourish their lives together.

'God be in their hearts and in their thinking'

that awareness of each others strengths and weaknesses will bring the joy of discovery, the thrill of growing togetherness and a unique oneness which only they two will know.

August 5th

Lord living in this community on the edge of a busy main road I often hear the sirens of emergency vehicles. Just as yesterday the sound of wedding bells brought joy to my heart and happy memories; this morning's peace was shattered by the piercing rudeness of sirens. Like a sharp stabbing pain they ripped through the tranquil air and were then gone. I have been thinking ever since about the poor souls caught up in a dreadful situation requiring ambulances and fire engines.

Father, thank you for ambulance and fire crews who have to deal with unimaginable carnage on a daily basis, keep them from harm as they tend to others.

I pray for those involved in road traffic accidents today and I pray for families who will hear upsetting news and for the people who will have to deliver it.

Lord may they all, professionals and injured, feel something of your comforting presence with them. May they really know the power of your love for them.

August 6th

Transfiguration of The Lord date in the Catholic calendar.

Matt17. 1-8 Mark 9:2-9; Luke 9:28-36

This is a tremendously powerful passage giving the disciples, and us through their writing, a glimpse of the glory of God. The vision of Moses and Elijah with Jesus are affirmation of the word of God made man and the confirmation of all that they themselves foretold. Recorded in the Old Testament, Moses wrote about the coming of a great prophet in Deuteronomy and Elijah heralded the arrival of the Messiah in Malachi.

We cannot be in any doubt about the profound effect this whole tableau would have had on Peter, James and John. The voice from heaven confirming that

'This is my son, whom I love: with him I am well pleased. Listen to him.'

I doubt I will experience anything approaching this sort of vision during my Christian life on earth but I thank God for this written record and those of Mark and Luke.

The confirmation that Jesus was, and is, the Son of God is overwhelming and my only possible response can be to adore and worship him.

Lord of the Transfiguration, Son of God, I honour and obey you.

August 7th

In the meditation of Mother Julian on the Revelations of Divine Love she writes about being tested by falling. Her explanation of the fall, the severity and distress of it, is its necessity in order for us to know our weakness and dependency on God.

She writes 'For if we never fell we should not know how weak and pitiable we are in ourselves. Nor should we fully know the wonderful love of our maker.' Enfolded in Love

Father for those in torment of pain or distress of mind I beseech your grace.

Lord for those brought low by situations beyond their control I beg your healing presence.

Lord Jesus may they, through their times of anguish, be brought to a place where deeper understanding and knowledge of you is their illumination and relief.

August 8th

Music can take one into the presence of God.

It can heal and soothe, it can delight and enchant.

It can lift one up high, to surf the clouds of heaven, in an expectation of seeing God.

It can bathe one in a sound so reassuringly familiar that one feels like a child safe in the arms of a favourite adult again.

It can bring memories of gloriously grand occasions or small, special, private ones, flooding back.

It can stir such distressing resonances that to cry is the only response.

Music transcends time and space.

Music takes us into the presence of God.

August 9th

I want to know more of you Lord.

I want to know more of the vast reservoir of goodness and wisdom which you have waiting for me and for all those who submit to your teaching.

Lord open my heart, eyes and mind today.

I don't want to miss anything which will lead me to a fuller understanding of your plan for me.

I don't want to miss anything which will lead me into a deeper knowledge of you.

I want to know more of you Lord, show me how.

Help me to make space, to look and listen for your presence, your teaching, your love.

I want to know more of you Lord.

August 10th

Lord of my heart, of my will and my life,

Thank you for only wanting my commitment to you.

Thank you that the gift of myself is all you want and all I need bring to this spiritual union.

August 11th

Gracious Lord thank you for another wonderful English summer day.

The rain overnight has left everywhere showered and refreshed to meet my early morning, appreciative inspection.

The air smells intoxicatingly pure and sweet and is clearer for having had the particles of pollen and dust damped down.

The colour in the flowers looks vibrant and they seem radiantly confident of their place in the borders.

The trees have lost their summer fatigue and their leaves no longer seem too heavy for the branches.

In fact the rain has watered everything and now here at least there is a pulsating energy again.

Oh I do appreciate things outside Lord. Thank you.

August 12th

'For all have sinned and fall short of the glory of God' Romans 3:23

Sin = Transgression
    Transgression = Wrongdoing
        Wrongdoing = Disobedience
            Disobedience = Misdemeanour

                    = Me

'But by the free gift of Gods grace all are put right with him through Jesus Christ.' Romans 3:24

God   **Jesus**   **Me**

Through the gift of the Son of God I can be free. Hallelujah.

Will I ever fully comprehend the true enormity of this gift?

August 13th

A sigh is a song to the Spirit
when it comes from a hopeless heart.
It's a prayer on the air to the heavens above
saying I'm just so human, thank God
You are love.
There aren't words to be heard,
nought worth saying,
repetition can seem awfully trite
but a sigh
and some silence
a touch
or a kiss
can convey in a second the
Lords special bliss
        and His balm
                and His peace
                      and His promise.

August 14th

Father your arrows were firing last night,
the heavens were like a battle royal with light
as we watched the shooting star showers.
Meteorites from distant shores
broke through to our world
exemplifying your unparalleled powers.
Flashes of brilliance as long as a blink
and as short as a glance caught our eyes
but their transience kept them unattainable
and despite our joy of the spectacle
left nothing but awe to our temporal beings.
From light years away in a place yet unknown
the Promethean pointers flew out,
cosmically entertaining us
at the same time reminding us
of our infinitesimal smallness.

August 15th

I always feel happy after seeing a shooting star. I have an eternal optimism, for a while at any rate. It is the same as seeing a rainbow. Something man, no matter how clever or professional or inventive; as yet, can have any part in making.

These are your phenomena great God of the universe.

I am always awestruck being able to witness them and to know that your hand spans time itself.

I cannot comprehend light years and their measure, I can barely appreciate their magnitude and it is even more than I can take in to realise that even then you are in control.

August 16th

What a lot of new vocabulary we have had to assimilate over the last couple of decades. I wonder what my grandma would make of it if she were to be able to hear.

Biodiversity, conservation, green as in the verb 'to be', global, solar, thermal, greenhouse as in gas, carbon tracking, genetics.

All of these words come under the heading of 'environmental' and what would she have known of her environment?

Good summers, less good summers; bad winters, mild winters, early spring, late spring, Indian summer, damp autumn, fogs, smog from coal fires before the clean air act of 1956.

Lord save me from becoming too anaesthetised to my responsibilities in the face of so much puzzling, and at times confrontational, language. Show me how best to play my part whilst still loving living in your world.

August 17th

When I came to proof read my work I found that I had missed this day out completely. There was an empty page with nothing written on it.

If I could choose one thing for today what would it be, what topic or thought, what bible verse or picture?

Shall I do some good deed in the neighbourhood or shall I write to someone I ought to have been in touch with ages ago?

Perhaps I'll garden or at least sit in it and enjoy the crossword from today's paper.

What would I do if I could 'write' a perfect day?

August 18th

When we pray we know that God hears.

Jesus prayed, forty days and forty nights at the start of his ministry; forty days and nights of seclusion and single minded devotion to prayer.

I know I should spend far more time in seclusion and prayer, not just catch hurried minutes during the day.

I know that only in prayerful seclusion will I be able to centre on the passionate and consuming love God wants me to comprehend.

I know that only by my own single minded devotion will I give my spirit the opportunity to touch the Spirit of the Living God.

Father open my heart to receive more of you through a growing determination to spend more time prayerfully in your company.

August 19th

I have had a post card this morning from a friend on holiday in Italy. It is a picture of the Michael Angelo 'Pieta.', the life sized sculpture of Mary holding the dead Christ in her arms.

The amazing thing about this piece of work is that Michael Angelo wanted to portray a youthful Mary, at peace, a contradiction to earlier artistic works which had shown the Holy Mother disfigured by grief.

As I look at the picture there is such serenity in the midst of deep, deep sorrow.

She is a testament to the support of a divine God whose will she lived her life in obedience to.

The majority of us, by God's grace, have not had to hold our beloved sons in this way and I can only wonder that Michael Angelo, at the tender age of twenty one, had the inspiration and maturity of understanding to assume such compliant peace for Mary.

I will treasure this card, not only for the message from a dear friend but to remind me of just how much our Heavenly Lord can support us if we live in submission to his will.

August 20th

Jesus prayed 'that all may be one, so that the world will believe.'
Jn17:21

How can we do this? How can we become **one** in the Christ like way of this prayer?

Perhaps we need to go back to the roots of what Jesus embodies.

Love.

Through love, through a deep love which is beyond words and cynicisms and ambiguities; which is beyond political correctness or social conventions.

Through love, where division of denomination and man made boundaries of liturgical individualism do not obscure the individual soul.

Through love, which builds communities of faith and trust, honour and integrity.

Through love, which is the only binding for us in our impoverished human weakness.

Then we will listen to the poor and the disenfranchised, then we will find a way to reconciliation and hope.

Then we will be **one.**

August 21st

You don't have to go to church to be Christian! How many times have I heard that phrase? And no, you don't except as I always answer, 'if you are, you want to'.

There is a lovely poem by Emily Dickinson
'Some Keep the Sabbath Going to Church' –

> Some keep the Sabbath going to church,
> I keep it staying at home
> with a bobolink for a chorister
> and an orchard for a dome.
> Some keep the Sabbath in surplice,
> I just wear my wings
> and instead of tolling the bell for church
> our little sexton sings.
> God preaches, a noted clergyman he
> and the sermon is never long,
> So instead of getting to heaven at last
> I'm going, all along.

Lord you reach me in all sorts of places and never more so than out of doors surrounded by your creation. The arguments about where one finds salvation still rumble on but in the final analysis salvation is a personal encounter, just me and God.

August 22nd

A fountain soars high into the air
and reflects in its droplets the changing colours
of the spectrum.
The once plain stream becomes a curtain
of momentary magic as it unfurls from on high
to delight.
As it tumbles in synchronised abandon to its
stone cistern, the music of the splatter plays in homage
to its entertaining majesty.
And a small shower borne on the gentle summer wind
refreshes captivated eyes as they follow the silver streamers
to their source.
And Christ is the fountain who soars over us all,
waiting for us to take around the thirsting world
his message.
A small shower to begin with, borne on a gentle breeze
to refresh and hydrate the tired essence of
a parched human race.
A small plain stream with the potential to explode
like a fountain into a torrent of astonishing
fulfilment.

August 23rd

Back to school preparations are going on all around us and trails of children and frazzled adults can be seen making uncooperative visits to shoe shops and the barbers. Feet that have spent the summer in sandals are being encased once more in sturdy leather, half a size too big. Hair which has been allowed to grow and turn amazingly sun kissed is being cut to regulation length. Parents are exchanging happy 'one week to go' glances across the heads of their little ones and trying to ignore the bored and belligerent sulks of adolescents.

What cost, in emotion and hard cash.

Lord as these rituals are happening I pray for the teachers getting ready to receive their new charges. May they be inspired to stimulate and encourage the new children in their care. May they feel energised and moved to meet the new school year with enthusiasm and passion and may they feel a renewed spirit of dedication within themselves.

August 24th

Matthew Mark Luke and John
Bless the bed that I lay on...
I can't remember any more of that childhood prayer but now I pray that
I might be
> filled with the messianic zeal of Matthew as I speak to others about Jesus.

That I might be
> as immediate and accessible as Mark in my discipleship.

That I might be
> clear and honest and prayerful like Luke in my dealings with others.

and that I might
> have the faith which John wants for every one of us.

"these are written that you may believe that Jesus is the Christ, the Son of God, and that believing you may have life in His name."   John 20:31

August 25th

Lord in simple and faithful trust I ask that through the direction of your word and the power of the Holy Spirit I might be able to take hold of, and espouse, the divine abilities of the four gospel writers. I read again yesterday's piece and think on each saint with reference to my own paltry efforts.

In my need Lord I kneel before you.

August 26th

God our Father, who through the gift of Jesus has become accessible to mortal man, may I revere you with all due respect.

May I never overstep the boundary which my veneration, of its own indebtedness, creates.

May I always be aware that in coming to you I am entering the Holy of Holies where over familiarity and matey language is inappropriate.

May I never, for one second, underestimate your omnipotence and the supremacy you have over all that lives.

Gracious Heavenly Lord hear my prayer.   Amen.

August 27th

A Bank Holiday and all the family have been here. It has been one of those days that couldn't be bettered. No atmospheres or undercurrents, from albeit loving factions, vying for attention; no irritable exchanges with impatient misunderstanding.

Lord it has been a grand day. There has been laughter and genuine celebration in the enjoyment we take and receive as a family.

There will always be differences of opinion; we are all adults with minds and thoughts which won't necessarily align.

There will always be more than one way to do something, especially where the rearing of children is concerned, or the way one person may or may not respond to another.

What matters is that we all pull together to make it work, that we all put self and selfish opinion to one side in favour of harmony and the greater good.

That has happened today and Lord I say 'thank you.'

August 28th

Tidying up from yesterday and reliving the antics of our grandson as I put his little red tractor away until next time.

Moving the extra garden chairs away and remembering the conversations and changes of dynamic as we moved from one topic to the next.

Looking at the red wine stain on a cloth and wondering if it will ever wash out, and you know Lord, I'm not sure I want it to. If it doesn't disappear it will serve as a permanent reminder of an expansive gesture of love which upset the glass in the first place.

I am not going to feel guilty that we had such a lovely day when so many people are lonely or without family, selfishly, I don't want to mar my happiness in this way. Is that wrong of me?

Lord I have an open, joyous appreciation of your bounteous goodness and I gratefully leave the rest to you.

August 29th

'The Thames barrier is a sign of Britain's vulnerability.'

Andrew Marr: The History of Modern Britain

This was said in the context of global warming and rising tide tables but it made me think about the other signs of our vulnerability.

Lord we need look no further than our own high streets, our own parks, our own communities to see how weak we are as a society.

Where are the gaps that need plugging in our own back yards?

Where are the gaps in the fence that allow precious lambs to be taken?

Where are our hearts impervious to exposed need, the helpless?

Why are our ears complacently deaf to defenceless cries for aid?

Is it possible that we all have an inbuilt Thames barrier?

August 30th

What an answer to prayer! After my soul searching of two days ago I found today's Bible verse was from Psalm 126 and I felt that it was perfectly acceptable in God's sight to be happy and without guilt.

'When the Lord brought us back to Jerusalem, it was like a dream.
How we laughed, how we sang for joy!
Then the other nations said about us
'The Lord did great things for them.'
Indeed he did great things for us:
how happy we were.
Lord take us back to our land,
Just as rain brings water back to dry river beds
Let those who wept as they sowed their seed
Gather the harvest with joy.
Those that wept as they went out carrying the seed
will come back singing for joy as they bring in the harvest.'

August 31st

I have been invited via a flier through the door to

'Make sure your funeral goes according to plan'.

I can pay for it in advance, thereby sparing my loved ones unnecessary worry and expense.

I can choose my plan for burial or cremation.

I can beat inflation by paying at today's prices.

I can pay in full or monthly instalments.

I can organise every detail to suit my wishes.

There was one thing missing -
>   the heaven or hell option.

September 1st

The Lord doesn't want an army of 'yes men' fighting on his side.

He wants questioning argument, and enquiring minds. He wants his soldiers to be constantly testing the boundaries of their faith, improving their knowledge and growing in the power of the spirit, through his grace.

He knows that faith which has been tested and assayed against secular opinion will make more convincing dialogue.

He wants his conscripts to be well informed and ready to stand in any arena as his men, for his cause.

The Lord doesn't want 'yes men' in his army.

He doesn't want blind adherence to anything.

The blind cannot see.

September 2nd

Well, that wasn't very politically correct was it? Yesterday I used a generic masculine form to refer to us all. Once upon a time I wouldn't have thought twice and certainly I personally never felt demeaned by such a use. Also, I hope that I haven't insulted any blind people by suggesting that because of their lack of sight they are incapable of making rational and well informed decisions. Clearly that was not my intent.

I thank the Lord that he can see straight into my heart and sentiments; that I don't have to couch everything I say to him in some prescribed grammatical form.

How much sincere, inspired and, maybe, controversial dialogue is lost to a watering down sentiment for pc's sake?

September 3rd

Holier than thou
    Self righteously pious
        Exhibiting an attitude of superior virtue
        Sanctimonious

Father God, protect me from any of the above accusations as I try to live my life for you.

Keep me grounded in the humble role of servant and aware only of your greatness.

Protect me, in your service, from the greed of position or importance.

Make my acknowledgement of your salvation a quiet strength rather than a cacophony.

Lead me in the ways of graciousness and modest bearing, showing only your gentility to everyone I meet.

September 4th

The Lord is my strength and my song, and He has become my salvation; He is my God, and I will praise Him.
    Exodus 15:2

This was the song of Moses, Miriam and the whole company of Israelites on their safe deliverance through the Red Sea.

Their chorus of thanksgiving to God must have been deafening.

Lord keep this song on my lips today I pray.

September 5th

Mountain - a symbol of faith, of triumph over adversity, of achievement.

"Those who trust in the Lord are like Mount Zion, which cannot be moved, but abides forever
Psalm 125:1:

Mount Sinai, the mountain upon which God gave Moses the Ten Commandments.

Mount Nebo from the top of which Moses was able to see the land which his people would inherit after his death.

In the New Testament, when Satan tempted Jesus, he took him to the top of a mountain, and showed him all the kingdoms of the world.

Jesus often went to the mountains to pray. On the night before he was crucified, he went into the Mount of Olives.

Mountains are tough, rugged and enduring, beautiful to look at with the early morning sun coming from behind them like a halo. Mesmerising in the evening light when set on fire before sunset.

To climb they present a challenge, but one worth taking.

At the top the view makes the assent worthwhile

The decent is aided by the adrenalin of achievement.

We need mountains in our lives to prove to ourselves that all things are possible through him who loves us.

September 6th

Today is my dear husband's birthday.

He is not a day older than when we met, in my eyes, though to some I guess he is now looking a little more wise and distinguished.

He is the same kind, gentle, loving, self effacing man he was all those years ago, except with the benefit of years he has become more so.

His compassion and concern for others, his integrity and joi d'vivre are what make him a man amongst men and I thank God daily for him.

Oh, and he is untidy and brings muck in from the garden on his boots, and leaves cupboard doors open, and can never find anything, and forgets when I tell him things!

Still, I adore him.

September 7th

I'm getting ready to go on holiday and it's always the same. I am full of excited anticipation but also a feeling of foreboding and a little unsettled at leaving my comfort zone.

I clean the house as though it were going up for sale and in case anyone has to come in in my absence.

I tidy drawers and make sure the beds are all made ready…for whom?

I wash everything in sight, as though washing machines might be deemed illegal during my separation from the laundry.

I usually depart a clapped out wreck from all the preparations.

Is it worth it? I ask myself as I go through my self inflicted ritual.

Well actually yes.

It means that at the other end, I come home to a perfectly presented house which won't need touching for awhile. Ergo, I get extra time once I am back and the holiday magic isn't lost immediately I come through the door.

Father thank you for the opportunity to have a holiday and change of scene. Thank you for our friends and neighbours who will look after the house, garden and hens whilst we are away and thank you for their prayerful cover during our travels.

September 8th

These are some of the headlines from today's papers.

'Celebrity status',' iconic role model', 'champion of the people', 'driver of the new world order'.

'Saviour of the side' – football.

'Peacemaker' – postal worker against strike action.

'Masters of the universe –tax breaks for the treasury',

'Take a chance for a lifetime's food bills paid' – a competition.

Wow, imagine what the headlines would be were Jesus to come back. Would there be such accreditation?

> 'Back on earth today an iconic role model and champion of the people. Give the celebrity status due to this driver of the 'New World Order', this saviour, this master of the universe. Enter our celebration competition to win a lifetimes supply of heavenly manna.'

Perhaps not; more likely,

> 'Gentle male, homeless, arrested for asking people to follow him, claiming to be the Messiah.'

September 9th

'I have complete confidence in the gospel' wrote Paul in his letter to the Romans, 'it is God's power to save all who believe. For the gospel reveals how God puts people right with himself: it is through faith from beginning to end.'

Here is the nub of my faith too.

Here is a message of salvation and life changing power, for anyone and everyone who will say yes to Jesus.

Lord help me concentrate on you and your will rather than on my inadequacies.

September 10th

Oh, how I could completely destroy myself by dwelling on my inadequacies.

The feeling of not being good enough, or able to, or capable of, or informed enough or…or….or!

I know that in the power of the Spirit and trusting in his all abiding presence and support, all things are possible and I am sorry for my lack of confidence, which is actually a lack of faith.

So Lord, send me out in the power of the Spirit to live and work to your glory.

September 11th

Enjoy the joy of knowing Jesus,
share his will with all whom you meet
and the place will be better,
the air will be sweeter,
you'll walk to a happier beat.

Enjoy the joy of knowing Jesus
bring his light to dark places here,
and the world will be lighter,
dull eyes will be brighter
the message of love will shine clear.

Enjoy the joy of Jesus
delight in his beauty and grace
and the elation you feel
will quite soon reveal
His amazing warmth and embrace.

September 12th

Lord as I hold this little cross, worn smooth by the hands that have gained so much comfort from it, I am aware of how much of their faith has penetrated its fabric.

How those hands, stroking the wood to the rhythm of their prayers, have left behind, in the patina, the imprint of strength gained and peace restored.

I feel my fingers folding round the off-set arms and see how naturally they fit into my hand and I wonder at how something so cruel and merciless could here be the symbol of love and forgiveness.

Lord as I leave this cross for the next prayerful pilgrim to hold, I pray that they too may experience the paradoxical beauty of your suffering and pain. That in this cross with its lopsided arms they will meet you and be revived.

September 13th

'Blessed assurance Jesus is mine'

Whoever has the Son has life; whoever does not have the Son of God does not have life.
>> 1John 5:12

I am writing this so that may know that you have eternal life – you that believe in the Son of God.
>> 1John 5:13

Blessed assurance, Jesus is mine.

This is my story, this is my song.

September 14th

Today I have earmarked for myself. I am going to read: nothing particularly uplifting or didactic, just a good murder mystery. I like the ones with lots of forensic detail.

I don't intend to clutter my mind by first trying to work or catch up with my emails. I am just going to take some time to transport myself into a world which has been prepared for me; a world where the table is set and the meal ready and waiting to be enjoyed.

I am going to surrender to an unfolding story from the pen of a master craftswoman and I am going to fall hook, line and sinker into the labyrinth of lies and deceit which she weaves. I will become inextricably bound up in a web of malpractice and duplicity.

Tomorrow I will be glad of normality and predictability and will be happy to resume my 'normal' life.

Thank you Father God for your hand on my life, which has made this day possible.

September 15th

I have been asked to pray for someone I don't know. A teenage daughter is perilously ill and her parents are the friends of my sister in Canada.

Words feel banal, trite and prosaic.

As a mother I can only imagine the dreadful heartache which the parents are going through. For my sister I feel her worry as she loves and supports her friends through this shocking and frightening time.

Yet what words can I offer in prayer for this situation, for these lovely people, for this staunchly Christian family?

I can't, I have none.

Lord God of healing and compassion, I sit with my hands open in total trust that you are with all those working to heal this young lady. May your will be done and may the darkness which surrounds them be turned to light.

September 16th

Words were insufficient yesterday. I felt completely bereft of oratory or written sentiment to express my feelings for my sister's friends.

I have thought about it a lot.

Heavenly Lord I know that even in the direst of circumstances it is alright just to come into your Holy presence and rest.

That coming to you, prayerfully, is more important than any wordy sentiments.

How gracious a teacher you are, how inept a pupil I am.

September 17th

'My dear friend, do not imitate what is bad but imitate what is good. Whoever does good belongs to God, whoever does what is bad has not seen God.' 3John 11

Where does that leave us on the days when we do neither?

When we don't get involved because we are being culpably negligent, deceitfully, stubbornly detached?

Where does that leave us?

What does it say about our commitment to a Gospel infused world, a Christ like ethic of concern?

We can comfort ourselves by knowing that we didn't do something really bad but we deceive ourselves if we try to argue away our apathy.

Lord I know that at times I get things wrong but I also know that like a parent you would rather we try than sit idly by.

September 18th

'Be endlessly humble in the face of truth and revelation,' I read that line once in a story about the American Civil War. It was said by a grandmother to her granddaughter. I know that the women of this time were expected to be endlessly humble in their demeanour and that to revere knowledge in someone, usually male, was a sign of great respect.

As I observe the way society moves today I feel that anything which highlights a lack of knowledge or information often leads to posturing and self defence in an anything but humble way.

Father thank you for the teachers you put before me daily. I pray that I might be always ready to be a scholar, to receive with gratitude that which is being revealed, from whatever, however unexpected, a source.

September 19th

Open my eyes
> to the possibilities of the Holy Spirit.

May I not
> confine them to the limits of my own understanding.

Open my heart
> to the possibilities of the Holy Spirit

May I blot out
> my preconceptions of the totality
>> about which I have no hope of ever
>> knowing in this life.

September 20th

Lord as I pray for and seek evidence of your divine will on my life I ask that I be saved from over analysing revelations of the Holy Spirit.

I can only diminish the wonder and incandescence of such experiences if I try to understand them too much, I merely end up weakening and reducing them to my own human ability.

Divine manifestation is beyond my amoebic language.

Let me be absorbed into the prayerful oneness of the still place with God and wait.

Ascension on the wings of numinous expectation will show me the face of my creator.

September 21st

It certainly felt like autumn today. There was a bank of leaves blown up against the hen house door and the ladies themselves were chattering and clucking, clearly discussing the needed refurbishment to their accommodation before the winter sets in.

It is impossible not to be cheered by the sight of these endearing little egg machines posturing and tossing their heads in acknowledgment of each other's observations. I feel they are having a very critical council about what I am wearing today but then I have been working in the garden and a selection of old sweaters and a hat seemed appropriate. I do smile at the looks I am getting from them though and think that perhaps tomorrow I should make a bit more effort, if only out of respect for the endless devotion they give to me through their continual bounty.

September 22nd

Yom Kippur - also known as the Day of Atonement. This is the Jewish day of repentance. For my Jewish friends it is one of the holiest and most solemn days of the year.

Its central theme is atonement from sins against both God and one's fellow man.

This is a great festival, the Holiest of the their year and is celebrated with fasting and prayer.

Lord as we Christians come before you at each service we pray the words of our confession and hear your great forgiveness through the words of the absolution.

May we all, Christian or Jew, who share the knowledge of the forgiving nature of our Father God, extend to each other such love, respect and understanding as He has taught us.

September 23rd

What a day!

I have had to prepare for a meeting which I wasn't looking forward to. I felt a sick empty hole in the middle of myself which no amount of common sense and 'good talking to' would quell.

I prayed for confidence; it wasn't there.

I prayed for peace, it didn't come.

I prayed for the right words to practice what I would say but there weren't any.

Then it was time to confront the situation. It was not an easy time but the Lord gave me the strength and self confidence needed to accomplish the task.

Sometimes I have to step out in faith before the power, for which I have so earnestly prayed, will be given.

Not until I commit, accepting that I might fail, will I be upheld.

September 24th

I am still thinking about yesterday and wondering how many other times I have castigated the Lord for not being there when I needed clear evidence of his presence!

How impatiently I have ploughed on thinking myself alone and forgotten, in a pit of despondency of my own making, of my own childish stupidity. The difference that I hope I now make is that, with prayerful hindsight I can acknowledge that I was never alone, not for one second and I am reminded of the prayer 'Footprints' by Mary Stevenson which closes with the lines:

LORD, you said that once I decided to follow
you, you'd walk with me all the way.
But I have noticed that during the most
troublesome times in my life,
there is only one set of footprints.
I don't understand why when
I needed you most you would leave me."
The LORD replied:
"My son, my precious child,
I love you and I would never leave you.

During your times of trial and suffering,
when you see only one set of footprints,
it was then that I carried you."

September 25th

If we follow where Christ leads we will often feel like
we are following a breeze
or an indeterminate essence.
We follow with hunger and curiosity
like children playing hide and seek in the forest.
The deeper we go, the greater the anticipation,
the greater the expectation.
Curiosity becomes fear, of the unknown,
like pushing on toothache to make the pain
seem deliciously worse, deliciously more daring.
If we follow where Christ leads we will often feel like
we are following the string of kite blowing away.
We know it is real but we can't quite catch it,
Still we keep on trying.
The more we try to be brave in the woods,
the longer we try to catch the string of the kite,
the more we learn about ourselves.
And all that we can be very sure of is that should we stumble,
fail or succeed,
Christ before me will become Christ within me.

September 26th

Heaven is my home and the earth my footstool.
What sort of house would you build for me?
Where is the place for me to live in?
Did I not make all these things? Acts 7:49/50

As I walked to post a letter this morning those verses seemed so appropriate. There was a wonderful East Anglia sky, blue, with great white meringue pillows blowing slowly across as if being wafted by the beat of angel wings, majestic yet gentle.

I walked home past a garden with the most striking display of dahlias, the colours were heart stoppingly perfect. It was a flawless kaleidoscope, daring the passer by not to notice.

It is a pitiably blinkered mind that would try and confine our God or the worship of him to set places or buildings.

Father keep me from any blindness of spirit which would compromise my vision of you.

September 27th

What a contrast today as I stood at a market stall in the East End of London on my way home from a meeting. Surrounded by buildings and traffic and more noises than I could identify, and yet there was yesterday's verse in my mind.

I saw it in the smiling faces of costermongers and customers; in the myriad vegetables and fruit spread like an organic quilt across stall after stall. Fruits I knew and some I didn't, vegetables familiar and strange, all set out with love and pride.

How could I ever choose one barrow from another? Which selection of good things to buy? I wanted to bring home far more food than was sensible; I wanted to recreate this piece of heaven in my kitchen.

The Lord asks

>'What sort of a home would you build for me?'

How can we improve on his perfection?

Market stall, clouds, flowers; the leaf of a pot plant, the rainbow of light through a raindrop.

I believe that wherever we sit and admire God's creation we are in his temple.

September 28th

I have decided that having a prayer life allows me a secret place. It gives me permission to withdraw from those around me with no explanation into a quiet and secluded space where I can meet God. This is well and fine because I am usually with sympathetic people who also appreciate the importance and necessity of prayer time. What I do is not in itself secret, they know where I am going; but once there, alone in my private space, what transpires is known only to God and me.

Is having a secret a bad thing?

I would not want to withhold something from general knowledge just for the sake of feeling a superior one-up man-ship. I do feel though that some things are mysteries which don't translate into the sound bite world which we now inhabit.

Prayer is a place which for many is the only space in the day they where they can be alone with their thoughts and I think of those living in towns and cities who often go to a church every day just to sit a while.

Prayer is the permission to develop our love affair with God, to feed on it and from it.

September 29th

Lord, when I rail at you like a spoilt child because my prayers are not being answered in the way I want them to be, I am then reduced to a tearfully apologetic and repentant mess.

I know that answers to prayer are not always immediate or spectacular; in fact more often than not they are a gentle, growing confidence in the rightness or wrongness of a situation. Maybe even a gradual realisation that what I was originally praying for is not the way you would have something be. Often the answer is so whispered, and because I am still petitioning, I miss it.

Forgive me for my impertinence I pray.

Forgive me for my greedy expectation of something which is your gracious gift alone.

September 30th

I'm drowning, drowning,
going down for the third time.
Send a submarine.
My life is flashing before me
as I go down through the weed and slime.
Send a submarine.
I didn't think I'd been **so** bad
but look at all things I'm sad about.
I'm drowning, drowning,
going down for the third time.
I thought I'd been a nice person,
a kind person, someone who cared
but now I see I chose the ones
I favoured with my time and tares.
My life is flashing before me
and it's not a pretty picture
but perhaps I'm only being shown
the situations where I should have
known better.
SOS, God save our souls.
Oh Lord reach down and grasp me,
pull me up and let me breathe again.
I'm being lifted, lifted
clear and then I hear through
the weed and slime,
'Come to me dear child of mine'.
Cancel the submarine, I'm saved.

October 1st

Autumn is officially here today. The musty air is heavy with damp undergrowth smells and there were mushrooms in the field. I don't much care for the prospect of winter. I'm an out-side sort of person, preferring to be grubbing about in the garden, where I do my best thinking. Then again if we didn't have the slowing down of this time of year we wouldn't have the spring and summer to look forward to and although our seasons are becoming blurred we can still approximate the months to a weather pattern.

I do enjoy the prospect of log fires and winter but that's because I love getting everything ready for Christmas. What a very shallow set of seasonal thoughts!

Oh Father God I am surrounded by the beauty of your earth and in whatever weather, whatever season, I give you all honour and glory that I am a part of your wonderful creation.

October 2nd

Is it contrived to try and put every situation one encounters into a gospel setting or is it merely living the gospel life?

Is it contrived to find an analogous biblical parable for every deed or exchange; or is it merely living the gospel life?

Perhaps the danger, if it is such, lies in over enthusiastic vocalising of our findings. Perhaps like Mary we should keep these things in our heart and ponder them there.

Perhaps through living the gospel life, having taken up the way of the cross, we can see in these moments of reflection the revelation, the fulfilling of the promises of Jesus to all who follow him.

For it is by God's grace that you have been saved through faith. It is not the result of your own efforts but God's gift so that no one can boast about it.
    Eph. 2:8-9

October 3rd

When people of other faiths meet and depart they extend the blessing of their God to their friend or colleague.

The Muslims say As sala'amu alaikum" - peace be upon you, and the generally expected reply is "walaikum as sala'am" - and unto you also, peace.

The Jewish faithful say Shalom – peace be with you.

In Hindu Namaste is said, accompanied by bringing together of the hands in a gesture of submission to another, in complete humility and service.

We say Good bye; it is a contraction of God be with you.

I think we who love the Lord should start to say 'God be with you' in full when we leave someone.

October 4th

'We believe in the Holy Spirit, the Lord and giver of life,
who proceeds from the Father and the Son,
who with the Father and the Son is worshipped and glorified,
who has spoken through the prophets.' The Creed.

Lord I was suddenly aware of the huge importance of that last line recently. There is an obvious appreciation of the Holy Spirit as having arrived at Pentecost, a theological statement of faith, when you, in your great mercy through Jesus, gave the power to Christians. Clearly though, your Spirit, the Spirit of God was the inspiration for the relationship between the Old Testament prophets and you. Also, given that it was your Spirit, it was holy. Psalm 51:13 'cast me not out from your presence and your Holy Spirit take not from me.' This may not be the Spirit of the Triune God, still to be revealed but the presence of God, the Spirit of God spoke through the prophets.

Praise be to God the Father and the Son and the Holy Spirit and thank you for the writers of our liturgy, from whom we can constantly learn.

October 5th

Loving Lord yet again, through your merciful love, and when I make a decent amount of time to study, you meet me at my point of need and more than fill me with the knowledge of your presence.

Keep me firm in my faith and reveal to me the mysteries of that faith as I grow day by day in your tender care. Amen

October 6th

'Carpenter seeks joiners'

Oh Lord, how corny is that?

Well it made me look. It made me think. It challenged me; if only because I'm not sure I would want that in the back of my car window.

Why not?

I am ashamed of my reaction.

What uncharitable thoughts, but I am still uncomfortable at the idea.

Who am I to feel embarrassed, uncomfortable, after what Jesus has done for me?

Print the stickers! I will atone for my arrogant and unchristian reaction to a gentle and loving invitation.

October 7th

Father I seek your direction. I seek clear understanding, that what I feel I am being led towards is very much your will and not my imagination.

Gracious Lord, whose generosity of care and compassion exceeds my human understanding, take me by the hand and lead me to the place where certainty removes doubt and conviction replaces qualms.

Open my heart to the possibilities of the challenges that a new direction would bring and answer my uncertainty.

Father in whose tender loving concern I have the utmost confidence, lead me to your will.

October 8th

Father help me to be on guard against using language which is inflammatory or condemnatory, albeit without intent to harm. It is so easy to put a bias on even simple comments and opinions. It is not always possible or necessary to be morally neutral and there are occasions where an opinion is sought. There are however, other times when a personal opinion should remain locked away inside until it has been paid the compliment of a little more evaluation and reason.

No one is perfect and with our flaws come our judgments and attitudes.

Father, help me I pray, to stay what I say until I have thought it through in the light of your grace.

October 9th

'Jesus, the Gift of Love.'

What a beautiful thought. This is the title of a treasured book of mine written by Jean Vanier, a man of faith and tremendous selfless service to the world of the handicapped.

Gifts are usually given with love, certainly with good wishes but here the gift is Jesus, who is love. Jesus from where the love of God for man was made humanly accessible.

How many times a day am I reminded of that great gift and its implications?

How magnanimous that God gave such a priceless treasure as his son Jesus, gave us a gift of his son Jesus, that we might have everlasting life.

How can I ever repay such generosity apart from by my total discipleship?

October 10th

Father the daughter of my sister's friends is now terminally ill and the miracle for which they have prayed is not likely to come. Not likely to come in the way of Jiarus's daughter at any rate.

I know prayer cover for the whole family has been gratefully received and warmly relied upon but the pain now in these sad, last days is beyond the imagination of many of us.

Your will be done Lord, and may the family and friends of this lovely young girl be upheld and strengthened. Only you can meet them and walk beside them. Only the reassuring message of eternal life in the arms of Jesus can sustain them.

In the name of Christ,   Amen.

October 11th

Laughter is infectious. I have just been with some six year olds who were busy playing but then started laughing. It was obviously a great secret from which we grown ups were excluded and developed into a fit of giggles which had all the children rolling around in genuine pleasure. Their mother tried to call the session to order, fearing that things would escalate into the inevitable tears but the merriment had really taken hold and no appeal to reason would calm things. It became evident that the adults, trying to be serious, were suppressing their mirth in support of the parent in charge. One by one however, we all succumbed to the universal language of laugher. It was a most spontaneously joyful quarter of an hour and left us all feeling as though we had taken a magic happiness potion.

Thank you for the gift of laughter Lord.

October 12

It isn't as if there isn't hope
for better times to come.
It isn't as though there isn't hope
for days when there will be sun again
to warm the heavy heart.
The wrap of misery will be shrugged off
for long enough to feel
the loving arms of Jesus
begin to heal the sore
places deep inside the heart
which seems to have atrophied
beyond redemption.
It isn't that there isn't hope,
it's just too dark to see today
the Light of the World still shining
waiting for the cloak to lift away
and reveal the peace.
The peace of the Lord
which the world cannot give.

October 13th

I must get on and do something with all the lavender heads I harvested at the beginning of August; they are collecting dust in an old washing-up bowl. I have often thought that I would like to have a go at distilling the oil from the flowers but recognise that I will never be able to amass all the tackle needed to do that in a domestic kitchen.

I love the way that when you squeeze the spikes the fragrance is released and there is always more to be enjoyed, even in old, dried ones. I think I am a bit like that in that when I let myself be pressed hard by the Holy Spirit, more potential is unlocked; more for the Lord to work with. Press me harder Lord.

October 14th

'Then I turned my thoughts to consider wisdom, and also madness and folly.'
Eccl. 2:12

Madness and folly seem to be reign supreme if one believes all that one reads in the papers day by day. Wisdom seems in short supply. This verse from the book of Ecclesiastes draws me back to the wisdom of the Old Testament and in particular to the teachings of Solomon.

True satisfaction will only ever come from knowing that we are living out God's purpose for us, from doing his will. This must be our ultimate goal and the challenges we face are a part of his plan for us. We will make more sense of the madness and folly we encounter along the way if we are grounded in our own objective.

Solomon closes his sermon by saying:-

'Now all has been heard and here is the conclusion of the matter: Fear God and keep his commandments, for this is the whole duty of every man. For God will bring every need into judgment including every hidden thing, whether good or evil.'
Eccl 12:13-14

October 15th

In the power of Christ I pray that the reading from yesterday might highlight to me the areas of my own days where I am lacking: Where I allow madness and folly to insidiously weave, with all reason, into my life, there to become an accepted part of the pattern. Lord open my eyes to the unnecessary distractions which are so attractive and which I have embraced, the things which are valueless and dispensable in my walk with you. Give me the wisdom to make sound judgements about things which will affect my learning more of you and which cloud my vision of the ultimate goal.

Lord in your mercy, hear my prayer.

October 16th

After feeling off colour for twenty four hours I have just had a piece of toast. Why is a slice of toast such comfort food? Why, when all else palls in the pantry, is a slice of toast so often just what the doctor ordered?

I appreciated it so much more than ever I do when it is made into a sandwich and the filling seems to be the main ingredient.

Just some toast with the lightest spread of butter.

What a simple banquet. Thank you for the delight it brought me Lord.

October 17th

This is the day of my dear departed sister's birthday. It never goes unnoticed and I think every year on the 'picture' a Christian friend gave to me shortly after her death.

I should add that she and all her family died together in an accident.

The picture I was given is a back view of the family, my sister and her husband, and their two little boys, running, laughing through an alpine meadow, away from the rest of us, free and very, very happy.

October 18th

I met a man the other day, from a non denominational group, who was going round our neighbourhood preaching about the Risen Christ. I couldn't get any straight answers to my very Anglican questions, even as I tried to assure him that the Risen Christ was also fundamental to the worshippers in our village, across the denominations. I was immediately suspicious of someone who claimed non denominational theology, multi denominational maybe but…. Anyway, I have been a bit bothered about how I dealt with the 'man from the ministry'. I am certain that I was friendly and open towards him but I have to admit to a quiet, unvoiced suspicion. I have been giving a lot of thought to my reaction and that of the majority of folks with whom I have spoken since. Then this morning as I was sitting working, I read Mark 9 38 - 40

"Teacher" said John, "we saw a man driving out demons in your name and we told him to stop because he was not one of us."

"Do not stop him" Jesus said. "No one who does a miracle in my name can in the next moment say anything bad about me, for whoever is not against us is for us.'"

October 19th

The Birds have been so noisy this afternoon. They have disturbed my work, disrupted it completely actually, because I had to do as they bid; stop and listen to them.

My bossy robin was sitting on the back of a garden chair directing operations and cocking a beady eye in my direction to make sure I was watching. The finches were bickering over the perches on the seed feeders and two large pigeons and several sparrows were arguing over who was going to have the spillages from the above.

As I watched a couple of blue tits flew onto the nut feeder and quietly had an early supper, completely oblivious to the avian bartering going on around them.

I know these birds neither reap nor do they store away in barns, and I know that I seem to spend a ridiculous amount of money of feeding them, which I suppose is still their Heavenly father feeding them through me (Matt.6:26) but it is a small price to pay for the joy they bring and the emotional impact they have on me as I watch them.

October 20th

From Lindisfarne to Canterbury,
Iona down to York,
From Walsingham to Saint Anne's on Sea
the Christian pilgrims pray and walk
and wait on Christ who is beside them.
From Hemel down to Horsham
and Brixton through to Hove
the communities of committed faith
support the pilgrims with their prayers
of intercessionary love.
From Salisbury's mighty spires to
to the cell of Mother Julian
the path of faith in the Lamb of God
is embedded firm by the feet which trod this land.
In Whitby as in Alton Hants
And Prinknash as in Buckden
The hands of holy houses pray
for all who set out on the way
of Christ.
This country is held in the mesh of God,
bound tight in the paths of faith,
sustained by holy chant and song
the verses of which are endless long
and the message strong to
serve Christ in one another
and love as he loves us.

October 21st

When I think about those holy feet from yesterday's prayers, and all the souls called by God to a life of service and prayer in convents, abbeys and monasteries up and down Great Britain, I realise how very small my contribution is. I realise that no matter how many hours I spend at the computer writing or how many quiet days I prepare for, there are people out there whose whole, every breathing, every waking moment is spent in open, total communion with God.

Then I think about the folks I get to talk to in the butchers, in the supermarket, at the play park with my grandsons and I remember and thank God for the myriad ways there are of being a servant.

Lord in your mercy, help me to blossom for you wherever I am pianted.

October 22nd

As if in confirmation of my prayer I found our table surrounded by unexpected guests last night. It had been a damp day and I had made a big stew, with some good beef and lots of vegetables from the garden. I had made a double batch thinking I would freeze some for later, when the call came and I realised that there had perhaps been someone with other ideas!

What pre-meal grace could possibly convey our eternal gratefulness for the joy of a surprise visit from dear friends with food and fellowship round the kitchen table where the Lord of Hosts is the guest of honour?

Thanks be to God.

October 23rd

'Father of all we give you thanks that when we were still far off you met us in your Son and brought us home.' I find these words from the closing prayer of the Family Eucharist service so powerful, so full of strength and sustenance.

The thought that when I was still far off, before I was here, God knew me, is tremendously affirming, and that through the saving power of Jesus Christ, he met me and brought me into the fold. Not only that but He will see me back safely to my heavenly home when the time comes. What a promise.

October 24th

The memorial day of Anthony Mary Claret the saint whose brother house of the order of the Claretians is here in the village of Buckden. Anthony was born in Salient in Catalonia, Spain, in 1807, the son of a weaver. He took up weaving but then studied for the priesthood, desiring to be a Jesuit. Ill health prevented his entering the Order, and he served as a secular priest. In 1849, he founded the Missionary Sons of the Immaculate Heart of Mary, known today as the Claretians. From 1850 to 1857 Anthony served as the archbishop of Santiago de Cuba. He returned to the court of Queen Isabella II as confessor, and went into exile with her in 1868. In 1869 and 1870, Anthony participated in the First Vatican Council. He died in the Cistercian monastery of Fontfroide in southern France on October 24, 1870. Anthony Mary Claret had the gift of prophecy and performed many miracles. The main mission of the brothers now is South America and Belize.

Lord I pray for all those in missionary work across your world today, I am in awe of their selflessness and faithfulness in following your call; their complete lack of personal self aggrandisement, seeking only to do your will is a real lesson.

October 25th

Father, as by your grace you saved me and gave me a new life in you, thank you for the reminder that we are all called to mission, wherever and whatever our place on earth. Thank you for reminding me that I have a task, a purpose, not just here at my desk in the comfort of my study as I write my prayers, but that I must also stretch myself beyond the comfort of this room to tell others about the Gospel of Christ, that they might come to know more of you and your saving power.   Amen.

October 26th

I met someone new last night at supper. I didn't know them at all, they were guests from Florida USA. I was immediately drawn to the lady and instantly felt as though I had known her for ever. These things do happen from time to time I know but this did feel to be almost three dimensional. In the course of the usual courteous, exploratory conversation it became clear that we shared many familial and professional similarities and we certainly had an appreciation of each others sense of humour. Then, one or other of us made a comment about our faith and we took off on the wings of the same Holy Spirit who empowers both our lives. She a Roman Catholic and I an Anglican were so immediately related through the love of Jesus that I have a new sister in Christ. How almighty and gracious is our God.

October 27th

Praise God in his sanctuary; praise him in his mighty heavens,
Praise him for his acts of power
Praise him for his surpassing greatness.   Ps 150:1-2

How big is surpassing?

It is beyond our human comprehension and therefore our vocabulary.

It exceeds, it is better than, it outdoes, it goes beyond.
It cannot be improved upon.

Hallelujah!

October 28th

My hands are an empty cup
on the end of my out stretched arms.
They hold the hope of reception and redemption
from all that harms and damages.
My hands are an empty cup
on the end of my out stretched arms
and they hold you up to the healing
embracing power of a sustaining spirit.
My hands are the hands of a woman
and mother
a wife
a sister
and friend
and they lend themselves gladly
to cradle gently your troubled soul.
You are in my hands and I cup them round your hurting,
You are in my hands and I draw you to me for warming
as a mother
a sister
and friend.

October 29th

Ps 150 'with trumpets harp and lyre, timbrel, pipe and cymbal'

So I let my hair down and danced, as the following verses of that same psalm bids.

I put on some music and

'Praised him with tambourine and dancing

Praise him with flute and strings

and harp and lyre

and resounding cymbals.'

I clapped and whirled around my kitchen in a joyous appreciation of God's unsurpassed greatness. I don't know what the postman thought; I didn't notice him till he was walking back down the driveway.

October 30th

Father of all, those who can physically dance and those who dance in their minds through the freedom of your love, help us to radiate the joy of knowing you.

Protect us from the oppressive, depressive elements which assail our faith daily and keep us dancing with delight at the untold joy of your presence in our lives.

October 31st

Witches and wizards
and pointed hats,
broomsticks and cauldrons
and one eyed cats.
Halloween jape or
Shakespeare's Hamlet?
Harmless fun or
dangerous playlet?
Faustian dalliance with
the antichrist or
innocent childhood
like white chocolate mice?

May the cross of Christ our Saviour protect the impressionable and curious from harm tonight.

November 1st

The Festival of All Saints. A feast celebrated in honour of all the saints, known and unknown.

I am guilty of not knowing as much about the lives of the saints as I perhaps should and certainly the more one reads the more one is inspired by the truly amazing lives they led and the things they accomplished.

Father, for all the saints who now rest with you in their celestial home thank you for the lives they led and the examples they were, and should still be to me.

For the power they have to hear and receive prayer and to intercede on my behalf I give grateful thanks and praise.

November 2nd

The festival of All Souls.

A day to reflect on the departed, mostly our loved ones but also those whose journey from our lives was perhaps less loving than it should have been. Those with whom we might have had 'unfinished business'. The apology never made, the apology never accepted; the guilt of things done or left undone; the burden of a stormy relationship never brought from enmity to peace.

A day to remember with gratitude those whose lives changed and moulded ours by their example, their guidance, their love and support.

Lord, as I remember those of my family now at peace with you, I pray for their continuing rest in your heaven. I ask forgiveness for those whom I let go away without first making things right and I give you praise for those whose lives were so very instrumental in giving me my loving upbringing. I pray for those who brought me to an open and living relationship with you and for all of them I ask your peace.

November 3rd

The magazines are now full of preparations for Christmas and how the various stars and luminaries in our society will be spending the 'Holidays'.

Well, first of all, to me it will always be the Festival of Christmas, not just another holiday and secondly what price Christmas without a true appreciation of the arrival of the Lamb of God? What inner contentment is brought, not bought, over and above the wrapping paper and bows when one knows what the Christ Child's arrival heralds, not just 2000 years ago but even today?

I love Christmas, I enjoy the preparations and choosing gifts and getting all the family home, of course I do but I can honestly say that the greatest gift I was ever given is Jesus in my life.

Lord may just one or two souls stop and wonder about the meaning of it all in the midst of these next few frenetic weeks. May just one or two of them see the cross of salvation in the crib and not just a lovely story.

November 4th

Christ, who feels our hurts and disappointments more keenly than we can ever imagine, walk with me today.

Show me your way in the clearest possible terms, that I might know without doubt that I am doing your will.

Dry my tears of frustrated ambition and bring me the peace of knowing that the rocks on your way, although hurtful when I fall, are there for good reason.

Help me to wait patiently for your guidance and to learn, always, the pleasure of serving you whether on rock strewn road or in sunny meadow.   2Cor.12: 9

November 5th

I love fireworks. Anyone who knows me knows I love fireworks.

The whole debate about the rights and wrongs, the political correctness, of Guy Fawkes Night does not compromise my enjoyment one bit. Perhaps it should.

The commemoration of the capture of, what today would be termed a terrorist, aka Guy Fawkes is a dubious pleasure but just like the fundamentalists of today he and his gang were likely, not representative of the whole body they claimed to personify, namely the Roman Catholic faith.

After the failed plot bonfires were set alight in celebration of the safe deliverance of the King and so Bonfire Night has less controversial connotations….in my mind.

Lord how easily I can find a way to suit my opinions, to substantiate my thoughts, to give credence to my opinions, to support my actions. How full of conceit am I?

November 6th

Lord As I walked the dog this morning the smell of cordite was still in the air, mixed with the faint whiff of fried onions from the hot-dog van. I remembered the sea of faces turned skyward, ooing and awing and gasping in admiration at each new explosion of pyrotechnic brilliance. The happiness and good natured community spirit was tangible and I couldn't help thinking that there should be another health warning on the side of fireworks explaining about the effects of the feel-good factor. If only that 'Essence of Good Nature' could be taken up for a few extra days, lived for a few extra hours, how might our neighbourhood, our town, our country, be strengthened? Lead us, Heavenly Father, Lead us.

November 7th

Sometimes I feel like I'm still at school. Like I have to keep being brought right back to the subject in hand and to be admonished when my mind strays and I end up day dreaming, staring into space. Then I am ashamed and remember the feeling of having let a favourite teacher down. It's as clear as yesterday that feeling.

My mind wandered like that today as I was having my quiet time. It was anywhere but on the bible notes and my thoughts took over my prayer time. I tried to focus but a kaleidoscope was zipping around my head and my eyes seamed to be dancing behind their closed lids.

I love the Lord and know that he loves me and I will rest in that knowledge and not try to make a forced and therefore weakened sacred space just now. Maybe this evening I will be able to come back into his arms in peace and then settle into a time of quite communion.

November 8th

Gracious Healer, I hold before you those who are hurting today. Those of my friends and acquaintances who have troubles and those I don't know personally but for whom I have been asked to pray.

Let your love flow through their pain,

Let your healing flow through their confusion,

Let your compassion flow through their discomfort,

Let your power lift them out of their confinement.

May you who are The Light of the World

shine into their suffering and illuminate their way through to your peace.
        Amen

November 9th

Father we can never know the reason why
our burdens are so heavy
but through our faith we know we have
another set of shoulders there
to lift the load and more than share
the weight.
Lord we cannot understand the motive
for our hurts
but through our faith we know we have
the arms of Jesus holding us steady
absorbing the grief and making us ready
for his healing.
For those with no faith but arms full of hurt
I pray more than for the saved,
It is they who need most the Saviour's love
and the feeling of being at peace and at rest
in the safety of our Lords restoring breast
for their healing.

November 10th

I was thinking about my spiritual roots this morning as I potted-on a couple of little cuttings I have been nurturing since the summer. I thought of the words of Paul to the Colossians:

'Keep your roots deep in him and build your lives on him and become stronger in your faith and be filled with thanksgiving,'   Col 2:6

These little plants are striving to survive but trusting me for their support and sustenance until they are mature enough to survive in the garden; even then they will require my guardianship to bring the best out in them.

I might be a bit old for the nursery bed but boy do I still need the protection and nurture afforded by my divine Head Gardener.

November 11th

Remembrance Day.

Lord it seems like all the souls who died in past wars died in vain. This world is as unstable and with more armed conflicts raging than ever. Brother is fighting brother; Sister is breeding hatred against sister. Mothers are holding dead sons and daughters in their arms.

The peace of the Lord is fathomless but seemingly only ever attainable, for the briefest time, in individual hearts.

How many of the conflicts across the ages have been about religion and how many about megalomania? How much religious conflict is actually about theology and how much about megalomania?

Remembrance Day. A day for the world to hang its head in shame.

November 12th

I have a resurrection hope after the soul searching of yesterday Father.

I have the knowledge that your cross bought the ultimate freedom, the ultimate peace and the ultimate justice.

This is affirming.

I have the knowledge that despite the bitter gall of war and killing, sadness and loss, I have the ambrosia of your indestructible, sustaining love.

This is sweetness.

I have the knowledge that evil, sin and destruction will never have the last word.

This is confidence.

May the risen Lord be always with all who recognise these truths.
Amen

November 13th

I made my Christmas cake this morning. I had a CD of Christmas music playing and the combination of the warm spicy smell, lovely familiar tunes and a general feeling that God's in His heaven all's right with the world, pervaded. Now five hours later the cake is cooling and the whole house is scented with festive baking. It's a safe, comforting smell, enriched with the expectation of the coming season. I'm glad I only make this mix on very special occasions so that I never tire of its uplifting promise.

November 14th

'The peace that Christ gives you is to guide you in the decisions that you make'

Col 3:15

Lord grant me the patience to wait on you and to seek that peace which is your confirmation to me that I do your will.

November 15th

Thank you Gracious Lord for this prayer of humble trust from Psalm 131, what comfort lies in these words.

Lord, I have given up my pride
 and turned away from my arrogance.
I am not concerned with great matters
or with subjects too difficult for me,
Instead I am content and at peace.
As a child lies quietly in its mother's arms,
 so my heart is quiet within me.
Israel, trust in the Lord
Now and forever.
Amen

November 16th

November 16 is the 320th day of the year (321st in leap years) in the Gregorian Calendar. There are 45 days remaining of this year and most importantly for me

It's my birthday!

Although I don't relish any of the associated problems of advancing years I am thankful that I live in a time where age is more and more of an irrelevance and one can believe oneself capable of anything one wants to do.

I think of the stately grand dames of my childhood, dressed in dark colours, living sedentary lives in the best armchair in the house and I compare them with my friends and I now; sweating it out at the gym, busy with work and leisure pursuits the whole week round; sharing and caring for elderly parents at one end of life and helping with grandchildren at the other.

Much has happened on the 16th November if one puts this date into the computer but of paramount importance; it's a happy day for me and thank you Lord for my life so far.

November 17th

I was given some book tokens yesterday and I am always thrilled with a gift like that. I probably won't spend them for weeks but they give me licence to go to the bookshops in Cambridge and browse for hours.

I will slowly work my way through the various categories, spending hours in the foreign travel section, day dreams a plenty there. Then to classical literature where I shall be reminded of all the unread masters I keep promising to tackle. I always spend far too much time in the cookery book shelves, some of them are also anthropological dissertations worth reading. Actually I just love the pictures of the food! Gardening, Poetry, Philosophy, World Religions, Geography....is there a book shop with a B&B attached?

Thank you for the lovely friend who gave me this precious present.

November 18th

Advertising is in full swing now for December 25th and as always my heart is heavy for the families trying to manage on not very much. The pain in the hearts of mothers as their children beseech them for the latest toy or trainers, the newest, most expensive piece of software or game is very present in my prayers.

Who are the moguls, in their ivory towers, pedalling this insincere marketing?

Amos (Old Testament) in the eight century BC wrote of the dangers of a consumer riddled society. He wrote about the complacency of the wealthy – 'fat-cats' as I think we would know them today, being so insincere behind their facades of faith and benevolence, that the injustice and oppression of the poor was made manifest. He called for justice to 'flow like a stream'.

Lord I can never begin to stop the train of the advertising industry but I can pray that there might be growing consciences in individuals in that industry who will stand up and be counted. Then might your 'justice flow'.

November 19th

School was out for the hens today. With little in the garden to hurt they were given free reign. They just didn't know which way to go and ran first one way then the other, bossy in their self importance; each thinking their companion had the better morsel. As I walked back up to the house just one of them followed me and I was convinced of her innate intelligence in remembering that those who knocked on the backdoor earlier in the year, before the spring closure, got a special treat. Hens are very fond of a few cornflakes, well, ok hens eat anything. How wise was she though, not to mess about dithering with the flock but to follow the source of something better? Father God, thank you that even through my hens you teach me and open my eyes to the constant lessons on offer.

November 20th

Christmas shopping this morning and then lunch with my daughters; Lord I try to be sensitive to the 'have nots', when it comes to children and I hope that I don't bore people rigid with talk of my own. Reading back through this year of devotions I don't think I have been too overindulgent but today I would just like to write how very blessed I am. We are all near enough to get together for the occasional lunch, usually with our two little grandsons as well and so after a morning all doing our own 'special bits' it was good to meet for a bowl of pasta and glass of wine. My two daughters are such fun to be with, I remember wondering if this would ever happen, when we were in the midst of teenage angst and hormones. We have a son too and a lovely daughter in law but they are less easy to get together with during the working day, we tend to go and see them for supper.

Father, whose family it is a privilege to be a part of, thank you for my own.

November 21st.

Perfect Lord, may all that I do today be acceptable in your sight.

Give me the wisdom to discern, before it is too late, any words or actions which would not be pleasing to you.

Grant me the breath of the Holy Spirit, to have the kind and gentle words that you might have used, whether in love or admonition.

And as I close my eyes on this day may I know that, although far from the perfection of the saints, I have given my best to your kingdom here on earth.

November 22nd

Less than a month to go to Christmas for us Christians, the festival of Diwali is happening now for our Hindu and Sikh neighbours and Hanukkah begins next week for the Jewish community. All these festivals are about light, light and goodness and a sincere belief in the inherent integrity of mankind.

The light which we as Christians welcome is a life changing experience and if all the light and goodness celebrated in the other faiths, by ordinary people, could be compounded, I honestly believe we could begin to turn this world around.

The light from so many hearts wanting only peace and harmony would shine through the cloudiest opinions, through the most divisive discourse.

November 23rd

How marvellous are your ways Father God. I am always moved at this time of year as I read the prophesies from the Old Testament about the coming of Christ. That Isaiah and Zechariah, Micah and Daniel, Jeremiah and Hosea, and a host of others, all foretold the arrival of the Messiah. How can anyone doubt the gospel truth when the provenance lies in hundreds of years of God given, documented prophesy?

Lord I am often too cynical to believe what I hear on the news and read in the papers but I am overawed by the evidence of prophetic messages about the coming of the Saviour of the world.

What are people still waiting for?

November 24th

We are going away for the week end. We are going to stay with dear friends and I am looking forward to it for very selfish reasons. 1. They live in a beautiful part of the country and we will doubtless have some good walks. 2. Lizzie is an excellent cook and so there will be some lovely meals. 3 They are both gracious hosts and make us feel like the most treasured company. 4. We all laugh a lot when we are together.

Last and by no means least, we share a love of the Lord Jesus who has been at the centre of our friendship from the day we all met.

So, selfish? No.

Immensely appreciative.

November 25th

'I will lift my eyes to the hills from whence comes my strength' Ps 121

I needed some of that strength to get to the top but as we walked and talked the climb was completed and the sense of achievement great.

It is good to get out to the hills and feel the timeless permanence of them restore some equilibrium to a very urban mindset, reaffirming the might of God's protection.

November 26th

After our walk yesterday we had a very delicious, lazy supper and then slipped into a companionable stupor, each deciding it was bed time but not having the strength to climb the stairs. We had been so motivated to conquer the hill in front of us earlier in the day, so empowered and thirsty for the challenge; now though, tired and relaxed we couldn't find an ounce more energy. What a wonderful feeling deeply earned tiredness is and what peace of mind in succumbing to it.

November 27th

Coals to Newcastle

Preaching to the converted

Teaching your grandmother to suck eggs

Can't teach an old dog new tricks

Well, Lord maybe a new bible was 'Coals to Newcastle' in this house but I am grateful to the friend who introduced me to it, with its inbuilt concordance I am taking a familiar walk with new glasses on..

Maybe it is 'Preaching to the converted' but it is deepening my understanding with its scholarly observations and information.

No it isn't teaching me what I already know, it is introducing me to new interpretations and understanding which have eluded me in that past.

Yes you can 'teach an old dog new tricks' if it is willing to learn.

November 28th

Lord, you can work change even in the hardest heart.

Grant me faithful patience to keep praying.

Grant me the blessed assurance that those for whom I pray are in your safe keeping, even if they themselves neither know nor acknowledge it yet.

And Grant me the wisdom to know that all things are possible through him who loves us, but, always in your time not mine.

What is impossible with men is possible with God. Luke 18:27

November 29th

'For I am the Lord your God who takes hold of your right hand and says to you

'do not fear I will help you'.' Is 41:13

Dear God of Isaiah you did help us. You sent your son, your precious son, to earth.

In this season of advent the stable place and the Holy Family is the major focus but I wonder today at you, a father, who can have a son and then sacrifice him.

It is an action that most parents cannot comprehend; it is we who would die for our children.

That is why you are God and we are mere mortals, the chasm between us could only ever have been bridged by something so divinely ordained; and you have been leading us by the hand ever since.

November 30th

St Andrew's Day and thank God for him. He was a disciple of John the Baptist and introduced Simon Peter, his brother, to Jesus. He was crucified for his faith, although not on a traditional cross which was deemed too good for him.

Yet again a saint is reminding me of the true meaning of discipleship. Yesterday I was thinking about a father figure, today I am thinking about the mother of those two boys. How did she feel at watching her young men leave their prosperous fishing business and both go off with someone called Jesus?

Lord for the saints I give thanks but I pray that the souls of their mothers may also be resting in your perpetual light.

December 1st

Great excitement in the kitchen this morning as the first window on the advent calendar was opened, now the countdown begins in earnest.

I am going into school today to share the children's assembly and looking forward to it. It is an interfaith school and there is always a deeply considerate balance drawn between the various groups. I marvel at, and admire, the teaching which brings all these precious little ones to a far greater understanding, acceptance and respect of each other's beliefs than many adults will ever reach. I pray that the foundation laid now will prosper far better understanding in the years to come.

    'and a little child will lead them .'   Is 12:6

December 2nd

'Who do people say I am?' Mk 8:27

Who do people say *I* am?

Who would be brave enough to ask this question?

Who would be totally prepared for what they might hear?

I've been thinking about this after I heard of a dinner party 'game' where the guests were asked to sum up the personalities of each other in one word!

A cruel game?

A fun game?

A disingenuous game?

Lord, am I prepared to hear who people say I am?

December 3rd

"A young Englishman of great towardness." This is part of the obituary of Thomas Spring, a seaman who perished in 1598.

'Of Great towardness', what a wonderful phrase.

As this year comes to a close I, in common with many people have already made inroads into next year's diary. Appointments which I am looking towards with anticipation.

I think though that the young seaman being so spoken of was a young man capable of being able to look in the direction of, for instance, right, from wrong. I feel that the words are applauding a maturity beyond his years; celebrating his ability to see what needed doing before it was evident. Here was a young man who had the powers of foresight almost, to contribute salient observations, a valuable part of the team playing strategies for managing life on an Elizabethan vessel; a young man with a thirst for the journey he was undertaking, a young man with a positive vision of the way ahead.

Lord may I go on my daily spiritual journey with

'great towardness'.

December 4th

I have just read a counter argument to the new study bible I was so excited about on November 27th. The article suggested that too much commentary is in fact a dilution to the point of uselessness, that exegesis leads to watering down which in turn means a weakening, a devaluation of the words. Well I haven't the teaching or intellectual capacity to rely totally on my own understanding and am grateful to those who share their knowledge. Prov 3:5

I have to say that I feel informed and enriched by the commentary in my new bible. However, I do understand and espouse the Lectio Divina approach of the Benedictines.

A slow, contemplation of one or two lines from a passage of scripture, repeated in open, prayerful expectation is indeed a divine way to absorb the word of God and from which to receive His teaching.

I believe that in both these situations our gracious Lord will meet me.

December 5th

Lord in your great goodness
       and with your infinite mercy
              and infinite patience,
I ask that you will still my soul.
Release me from the straightjacket in which I have bound myself.
Free me from the bondage of my organisation and routine.

Silence my heart and mind and lay them open to receive your will for me.
Silence my heart and mind and lay them open to receive.
Silence my heart and mind and lay them open.
Silence my heart and mind.
Silence.

December 6th

Lots of Christmas Carols, on the radio, in the shops and in the house and I indulge in an orgy of seasonal, musical, sentimentality.

I love it.

I am not going to spoil my advent anticipation with the shadow of Easter; time will bring that along soon enough.

I am not going to 'bah humbug' my way past the choir of children in the precinct.

I am thrilled and delighted to be getting ready for the festival which celebrates the beginning of mankind's salvation. I accept, with some reluctance, the over commercialisation and the loss of the message but…..

…….as people go around humming a familiar tune, singing words they learnt in childhood, they are acknowledging the Lord. They are, however fleetingly, taking part in the miracle, that is the nativity.

The best bit of all is the Salvation Army Band and I will go out of my way to stand and listen to them.

Ding Dong merrily on High!

December 7th

How transformed has my life been by the love of Christ, this week, this month, this year, across the years?

There have been great high spots, where I have felt I was soaring with the saints and angels, as certain projects and ministries saw the light of day and were well received.

There have been dry and dusty periods in the wilderness when I felt far from the glory of God.

I know though, that my life has been transformed by the love of Christ when I realise that my very first reaction in any situation is to pray. Whether in grateful adoration or as a cry for help my first thought, my first words are with my Lord.

May the transforming power of the love of Christ, and the purification of my soul by his most precious blood, be a continuing refining in me until I see Him face to face.

December 8th

Advent and Lent, two forty day periods of reflection in the Divine calendar .

In Eastern Orthodox churches Advent is actually called Winter Lent or the Nativity Fast.

In common with Christians the world over I try to make a committed Lenten pilgrimage of prayer and study for the 40 days and 40 nights.

In common with Christians the world over I suspect, I do not make the same devotional journey through Advent.

Perhaps I should.

The cleansing which precedes Easter Sunday makes the resurrection morning so much brighter.

Would a rather more contemplative and spiritual walk through advent make the lights of Christmas morning even more intense for me? Oh yes.

December 9th

In the Bleak Midwinter...................not this year! It is so unseasonably warm and the pundits of doom and gloom are full of their prognostications about the way in which we are ruining the world.

Father God whose mighty arm can more than span the globe, forgive us when we mistreat your beautiful world. As our awareness of things we can do to help the planet increases, meet us in our efforts I pray and restore some equilibrium to the whole debate about global warming.

December 10th

"What would you like for Christmas Darling"
"I don't really know, what would *you* like"
Peace in the world,
An end to starvation and want,
An arms embargo,
Clean water, sanitation and education for everyone.
Yes, all of those please.
Perhaps for Christmas I would like some notion that something good is happening somewhere.

Some notion that the hard work of aid agencies and genuinely good people is beginning to make a difference.

Some notion that the gift of the Christ Child to mankind is being lived out in a real and positive way today, now.

Some notion that through the power of the Holy Spirit real change is becoming manifest.

December 11th

On the road
in a barn
where the animals lay
is the place where the world finds
redemption.
An inauspicious start
from where
to begin the journey of a
lifetime which ends on a
cross.
Such a meagre way
for us to learn how to see
how poor we would be without
the gospel prince and his
kingdom.
Look hard in the straw
in the dirt, smell the smell
of the place he was born
and be sure to acknowledge the
King.
On the road
when we meet the reduced and
deprived and the broken and destitute souls
we will if we learn how to see,
see Christ.

December 12th

It is fatal, it should carry a health warning, or maybe it should be timed not to open until Christmas Eve!

We are like children when there is chocolate in the house, which is why we can't really be trusted for most of the year to be responsible.

I bought a big tin of Cadbury's Roses and opened them to fill up the pockets on the advent calendar. I then put them away ....except I knew where I had put them and so did someone else!

So with almost a fortnight still to go to the festivities we are half way through the tin and all our favourite ones are already gone.

It is so easy to be benevolent with oneself and so indulgent with the ones we love and yet I know I don't always extend those sentiments so generously to others.

Lord teach me to let you be the arbiter of situations about which I know little or nothing and help me to treat everyone with the justice I metre out for me and mine.

December 13th

Our wedding anniversary. It seems a long time since the foggy morning in 1969 when we had, by today's standards, a very simple wedding. My 'in-laws to be' car broke down crossing the moors from Yorkshire to Cheshire and I was waiting like a cat on a hot tin roof in the porch of the church for nearly half an hour. No mobile phones to keep us in the picture. My Father was all for getting on with it, his unseemly haste at getting me off his hands was in sympathy with my own feelings of wanting to 'get on with it' however, the dear Minister breathed calm and great deal of prayer over the situation. Eventually his faith was rewarded, Mother and Father-in-law arrived, very distressed, and we had a wedding.

We are still here, and more compatible with each passing year, primarily as I acknowledge because 'he' is so patient and because I have not as yet taken up knife throwing. We have laughed and cried our way through crisis and predicament and come out stronger, we have the bond of faith which binds us with love and understanding and the Lord is ever present in all that we do and say.

December 14th

Let the words of repeated and familiar prayer sink slowly into your heart and disperse through your system, like a cube of sugar slowly disintegrating in a glass of tea.

Say the words of comfort over and over again, gently allowing the substance of the meaning to penetrate beyond your known self, to the place where God is in you.

God is prayer and in prayer.

December 15th

Father as I prepare to lead a quiet day I ask that you will meet me with all my hopes and expectation, and empower me to facilitate a wonderful day for everyone.

Thank you for the leading of your Holy Spirit during my compilation of the material and for your answer to prayer in giving me inspiration.

Open the hearts of those coming to hear your words for them alone, make their time in retreat a personal encounter with their Lord.

Fill to overflowing the thirsty and tired souls whose time with you recently has been scarce.

Move in the minds of those whose journey with you has been on rocky ground in this past year and Father God fling wide the door to those who hear your knocking and invite you in.

No matter what state or place we find ourselves personally, we will come in faithful anticipation and belief that you will minister to us.

Lord here I am, send me.   Is 6: 8

December 16th

Thank you for the tangible feeling of spirit filled love which remains in the house after a quiet day. Every room was used and prayed in and the tranquillity which people found as they opened themselves to your power seems suspended in the air. It is, for a brief moment in time, like the serenity one finds in a cloister or holy place where the faithful have met with God for many centuries.

I sit in your awesome presence and place my spirit in your hands, aware of your fingerprints all around me.

December 17th

Travel brochures. This is where I began the year, being promised a glimpse of paradise!

How interesting that the journey through the hell of the present transport restrictions in airports, industrial actions by baggage handlers and general holiday mayhem will 'pale into insignificance once paradise is reached'.

That's Life!

The difference between the commercial state and the heavenly one is that there are only immigration, security checks and customs to pass through. No God to answer to. There are no questions asked of ones faithfulness in order to embark on the journey or to be received into the country of choice. No inspection of ones previous life…criminality excepting. The only mitigating factor is whether one has enough money to pay for it.

It's really much easier to travel to the heavenly paradise; certainly there won't be any weight restrictions! Nothing to pack and no amount of money will buy a ticket.

Thank God I said 'yes' to Jesus, that I acknowledged him as my Risen Lord.

A glimpse of paradise? I'll wait til I can experience it in all its glory!

December 18th

I read the King James Bible today and was immediately draw into the beauty of the text. The comfort of those words brings such warmth and deep reverence to me. Years of Sunday School teaching I suppose, years of learning passages of the bible for scripture competitions and exams. Rather like the poetry one learned in school and can still recite many years later, bible verses are etched in my memory and can be recalled, chapter and verse. I don't think I really knew the meaning or the implication behind half of what I was trying to memorise at the time but I am so grateful now that I did.

Modern translations have made the text more accessible to modern man, more understandable and God more approachable and that it good. But, just as liturgical prayer takes one's thoughts away from self and into God so, for me the text of the King James Bible seems to re-orientate me with my maker.

'For whatsoever things were written aforetime were written for our learning, that we through patience and comfort of the scriptures might have hope.
Romans 15:4

December 19th

Dear Mary, Mother of our Lord, I gratefully acknowledge the journey which you undertook on my behalf all those many years ago. I think of the agony and indignity you suffered, heavily pregnant; travelling all the way from Nazareth to Bethlehem, along rutted tracks and uneven surfaces. I think of the miles you covered wondering and worrying about your precious unborn baby, as any mother would. The fact that you knew you were carrying the Son of God must have increased your concern unbearably. It is 70 miles from Nazareth to Bethlehem so I imagine you would be setting off about now. Gracious Mary, Holy Mother, Deo Gratias.

December 20th

A favourite prayer from The Book of Common Prayer: The third Collect for Grace.

O Lord our heavenly Father, Almighty and everlasting God, who hast safely brought us to the beginning of this day; defend us in the same with thy mighty power, and grant that this day we fall into no sin neither run into any kind of danger; but that all our doings may be ordered by thy governance, to do always what is righteous in thy sight, through Jesus Christ our Lord. Amen.

December 21st

"Happy Holiday" the postman greeted me as I took in a parcel this morning. NO!

Happy Christmas, please.

He was being politically correct. They have probably all had training about how not to offend any particular creed.

I am offended though. I am offended that my festival, my celebration has been wiped away, and in so being, threatening also the festivals and celebrations of my Jewish, Muslim and Hindu friends.

Lord in your great heaven, where can we go for guidance which neither patronises nor marginalises but respects and enriches our multi faith society.

December 22nd

Lord, what will you have to fill my days next? At the end of this year I will have completed this little book of devotions. I am not at the end of the journey yet but I am anxious to know what is coming afterwards. Like my elderly friend who was always more interested in pudding than the main course.

I know that what ever you have planned it will be a challenge but that there will be great joy in knowing that I am using the days as you will me.

So I keep watch, and listen and wait, knowing that when it comes, your work for me will be a holy command which I will endeavour to fulfil.

December 23rd

I have been to Cambridge to do a few last minute bits of shopping. The market place looked magical with all the lights on the stalls twinkling in the cold afternoon air. There was good nature and bonhomie in abundance and cheeky traders asking for a Christmas kiss under their oversized bunches of mistletoe. One guy was giving out tangerines to the children, which was an amazing gesture of festive generosity and another was teasing them about how many days they had to be good until Santa came. Several old ladies were being given a rousing chorus of 'Hark the herald' by a fruit and veg. man, then they joined in and the folk around them did. It was a spontaneous moment of sheer joy.

I know I grouse about the Christian message of Christmas being lost in a frenzy of consumerism but today in the market the love which came at Christmas was everywhere. Gentle Jesus thank you.

December 24th

Lord I come before you today with a full and grateful heart. I ask for you to be very present in our home for the next couple of weeks as family and friends come to stay and share the Christmas festivities.

May we all have the tolerance needed to support each other as the days pass in love, laughter and tired tears.

May we remember the reason for our getting together, the arrival of your Kingship here on earth .

And tonight, as we celebrate another glorious happy Christmas in our ever growing family, send to us anyone who you want us to be sharing the days with.

Later on, with the little ones tucked up in bed, those of us who can, will go to midnight communion. On this special night we will gather in church to wait for your glorious Christmas morning and the Son of Man, the Saviour of the World will be reaffirmed in us all.

December 25th

You're here, you came!
How wonderful to see you!
How was the journey?
Can you stay long?
Forever
Why, that's amazing!
Where will you stay?
In peoples hearts
How will you do that?
Because you'll die!
But you only just got here.
So you came and then you'll go
and then you'll be with us in spirit
until you come again?
Will I know that you are always with me?
Always and Forever?
Oh, that's alright then.

December 26th

The Lord says

"Here is my servant whom I strengthen, the one I have chosen and with whom I am pleased.

I have filled him with my spirit and he will bring justice to every nation.

He will not shout nor raise his voice or make loud speeches in the streets.

He will not break off a bent reed or put out a flickering lamp.

He will bring lasting justice to all.

He will not loose courage; he will establish justice on the earth.

Distant lands wait eagerly for his teaching."

Is 42:1-4

December 27th

To enter into the communion with God which was made possible in the Christ Child one needs time.

I have time this morning, everyone has gone for a walk to the woods with the dog. I have rushed my time with you the last few days. I have rushed into the meal without even stopping to wash my hands, eaten with unseemly haste and rushed off again. The ingredients which made a fine dish have been wasted on me. A time of very special sharing has been lost and the ultimate enjoyment and appreciation less than satisfactory. So Lord I come and sit quietly beside your crib, gazing on your beauty and thinking on all that you being here means.

Sorry about the food allegory Lord, I've obviously been doing a lot of cooking.

December 28th

The end of the year and the end of this journey on paper are drawing ever nearer. I want neither to finish. The year has been good, with few real upsets and lots to remember with fondness. My daily time at the computer with this prayer diary has been, at times; a walk to clear my mind and straighten out my thoughts, a time of letting off steam or of giving thanks but always, a walk of faith. I have gained wonderful insights into passages of scripture which I had never really looked at before and enjoyed a closeness with God which making the time has brought me.

Lord I wish I knew what you have in store for me next, but then I wouldn't be stepping out in faith.

December 29th

Another party Lord, how you must despair of the social whirl we get caught up in at this time of year. However, you gave us the human ability to register enjoyment and to appreciate company so in very thinly veiled terms I feel I am living out the generosity of life which you made me for. There will be days ahead yet, in the dark winter still to come, when these times will be like bright lights to be remembered and revisited, when the warmth and companionship shared will be a blanket of hope for spring and more happy meetings. So, thank you for the parties, I am loving them all.

December 30th

A sad day in my heart Father, lots of busy preparation for our visitors later this afternoon but a sad feeling inside. I am not a Hogmanay fan, as much as I enjoy a party. I always feel melancholic approaching New Years Eve and I don't really know why, it's been the same since I was very little and allowed to stay up for the first time.

I won't let it transmit to anyone else. I suppose it's insecurity in not knowing what the future holds.

Shouldn't all that really matters be that whatever it holds, you are there with me?

Oh yes, of that I am certain.

December 31st

Loving Lord, into your keeping I place all those I love and pray for. I give you thanks and praise for your greatness and I treasure the certain knowledge that in you I will find salvation and my ultimate eternal rest.

Go before me into this coming year and may my feet be as swift to do your will as you are to support and guide me.

The Grace of the Lord Jesus and the love of God and the fellowship of the Holy Spirit be with us all evermore. Amen.